CITYSPOTS
NAPLES

Ryan Levitt

Written by Ryan Levitt
Original photography by Neil Setchfield
Front cover photography © Martin Moos/Lonely Planet Images
Series design based on an original concept by Studio 183 Limited

Produced by Cambridge Publishing Management Limited
Project Editor: Rachel Wood
Layout: Julie Crane
Maps: PC Graphics
Transport map: © Communicarta Ltd

Published by Thomas Cook Publishing
A division of Thomas Cook Tour Operations Limited
Company Registration No. 1450464 England
PO Box 227, Unit 18, Coningsby Road
Peterborough PE3 8SB, United Kingdom
email: books@thomascook.com
www.thomascookpublishing.com
+ 44 (0) 1733 416477

ISBN-13: 978-1-84157-638-1
ISBN-10: 1-84157-638-7

First edition © 2006 Thomas Cook Publishing
Text © 2006 Thomas Cook Publishing
Maps © 2006 Thomas Cook Publishing
Series Editor: Kelly Anne Pipes
Project Editor: Diane Ashmore
Production/DTP: Steven Collins

Printed and bound in Spain by GraphyCems

CONTENTS

SYMBOLS & ABBREVIATIONS

The following symbols are used throughout this book:

ⓐ address ① telephone ① fax ⓔ email ⓦ website address
① opening times Ⓝ public transport connections ① important

The following symbols are used on the maps:

ℹ️ information office	○ city
airport	○ large town
➕ hospital	○ small town
police station	= motorway
bus station	— main road
railway station	minor road
Ⓜ metro	— railway
cathedral	
❶ numbers denote featured cafés & restaurants	

Hotels and restaurants are graded by approximate price as follows:
£ budget ££ mid-range £££ expensive

▶ *The elegant Piazza Plebiscito*

Introduction

Milan has the money, Florence the art, Venice the water and Rome the power, but Naples? Well, Naples has the heart. Gateway to the South, Naples is Italy's most spirited city. Over the centuries,

⬢ *The atmospheric streets of Spaccanapoli*

countless cultures have laid claim to this glowing metropolis, yet none has held power over it for too long. It is the mighty Mount Vesuvius that forever controls the fate of this bustling port, overshadowing the region with the threat of destruction.

A visit to Naples is like a step back in time to the days when children played with sticks and balls, mothers heard and saw everything and family meals meant that entire communities shut down for Sunday dinner. Shopping and sophistication it may lack, but for a sense of 'real' Italy, you can't beat Naples.

For many years, Naples was considered a no-go area. This reputation as a crime-ridden city has largely been erased following various high-profile anti-corruption campaigns that dominated the headlines during much of the 1990s. The result is a destination that is working better than ever. Yes, there are still the garbage strikes and choking traffic problems, but a metro system is beginning to make headway and a sense of pride that hasn't been seen since before World War II is starting to creep back.

Even the UNESCO World Heritage Sites of Herculaneum and Pompeii are experiencing a resurgence of interest, as debate rages on how best to maintain the remains for the visitors of tomorrow.

Naples peaks in popularity during the summer months when it becomes the gateway to Capri, Ischia and the Amalfi Coast. Too many travellers ignore the trappings of Naples, preferring instead to hop on the first ferry out of town. To do this is to ignore some of the finest dining possibilities, cutting-edge modern art and colourful markets in the country.

Lying on the beach may top up the tan but nothing beats a Campari in the Piazza Bellini following a long day of church exploring. Even the splutter of the passing Vespas sounds different in this, Italy's most vibrant of towns.

When to go

With its Mediterranean climate, Naples is a great place to visit at any time of the year. Winter is considered to be the most inhospitable period, when ferry schedules are curtailed, fog occasionally sets in and streets can be chilly and damp – but for atmosphere, quiet streets and nights to ramble through undisturbed, the city reveals secrets on every corner during this season.

While summers draw the bulk of the crowds, most visitors make a beeline to the islands and Amalfi Coast due to the heat and humidity. Much of the city closes down during August so it is best to check in advance whether the shops, restaurants and museums you want to see will be open during your stay. Great weather and a calendar of intriguing religious and social events make May, September and October wonderful months to consider a trip.

⬤ *Springtime at the Villa Communale*

SEASONS & CLIMATE

Temperatures in Naples can range from as high as 40°C (104°F) at the height of the summer, to as low as 0°C (32°F) during the bleaker months of December and January. During July and August many locals head to country retreats or to family properties on Procida, Ischia or Capri in order to take advantage of the cooling island breezes.

Between May and September, rainfall is minimal, averaging at about 15 mm (½ in) per month. From September onwards, dampness sets in, reaching a peak in mid-November.

ANNUAL EVENTS

Neapolitans are extremely religious and superstitious. As such, there are literally hundreds of events and processions in the city throughout the year. Exact dates change, so it is best to confirm dates before making any reservations. The Osservatorio Turistico-Culturale in the Piazza del Plebiscito is a great resource regarding what's on. Check out the Osservatorio website (ⓦ www.inaples.it).

January
La Befana is the Neapolitan version of Santa Claus. An old hag descends from the sky to bring gifts to good children and leave charcoal for bad ones. The distribution occurs in the Piazza del Plebiscito on 6 January.

February/March
Galassia Gutenburg Southern Italy's largest book fair. ☎ 081 320 3181 ⓦ www.galassia.org
Carnevale Naples' last chance for a party before Easter. Residents relax knowing they'll soon have to endure the depression of Lent. ☎ 081 247 1123

March

Benvenuta Primavera Uncover the secret squares and gardens of Naples during this month-long collection of guided tours and theatrical happenings scattered throughout the city. ☎ 081 247 1123

April

Settimana per la cultura Italy opens its museums free of charge for one week. Many venues extend opening hours in order to accommodate the crowds. ☎ 800 991 199 ⓦ www.beniculturali.it

May

Maggio dei Monumenti Naples' largest free cultural festival offers up a vast array of events and opens some sites that have been locked for decades. ☎ 081 247 1123

Napoli Marathon Three distances to choose from: the full marathon; a five-kilometre (three-mile) challenge; or a leisurely walk. ⓦ www.napolimarathon.it

June to September

Estate a Napoli Open-air films, theatre and music all summer. ☎ 081 247 1123

July

Neapolis Festival Southern Italy's largest international rock festival. Previous performers include Jamiroquai, Aerosmith and Lenny Kravitz. ⓦ www.neapolis.it

Santa Maria del Carmine The bell tower of the Santa Maria del Carmine church is 'blown up' by fireworks in a spectacular display every 16 July.

August

Ferragosto The Feast of the Assumption is celebrated on 15 August throughout the region. A slippery pole competition is the highlight of the festivities in Pozzuoli.

September

Feast of San Gennaro Naples' patron saint shuts the city every year on 19 September. A vial of San Gennaro's blood liquefies as frantic praying in the *duomo* surrounds the precious artefact.

December

Natale (Christmas) Churches bring out their nativity scenes, shoppers bustle along San Gregorio Armeno and concerts of sacred music occur every evening. A magical time of year.

Capodanno (New Year's Eve) Neapolitans ring in the New Year at a packed concert of classical, rock and traditional music in the Piazza del Plebiscito.

PUBLIC HOLIDAYS

New Year's Day 1 January

Epiphany 6 January

Easter Monday

Liberation Day 25 April

Labour Day 1 May

Republic Day 2 June

Feast of the Assumption
  15 August

All Saints' Day 1 November

**Feast of the Immaculate
  Conception** 8 December

Christmas Day
  25 December

Boxing Day 26 December

Feast of San Gennaro

Every year on 19 September, Naples screeches to a halt as superstition, devotion and religious fervour whip city residents into a frenzy of prayer. It is on this day that the blood of the city's patron saint, San Gennaro, liquefies as black-clad widows and seemingly conservative residents gather together at the *duomo* (cathedral) to urge on the process.

The length of time it takes for the blood to liquefy – it has taken everything from two minutes to two hours in the recent past – determines what the future year has in store for residents, with everything from Vesuvius' eruptions to the success (or failure) of the local football team blamed on the annual ritual.

San Gennaro met his untimely end in the year 305 when he was beheaded in the *Solfatara* (sulphur mines). His blood was collected by a pious woman named Eusabia and brought to the catacombs of San Gennaro. The first occurrence involving the liquefaction of his blood happened about a century later.

Today, San Gennaro's blood can be seen bubbling on three days throughout the year: the Saturday before the first Sunday in May, the feast day on 19 September and on 16 December. While crowds surround the blood on each of the days, it is only on the feast day when the future is foretold.

Loved by local residents, San Gennaro hasn't always been as popular with the Vatican. During the Second Vatican Council of the 1960s, San Gennaro was downgraded from saint to local cult, resulting in widespread graffiti protests and demonstrations. Pope John Paul II officially reinstated San Gennaro to his position in 1980. As a result, the former Pope was adored by Neapolitans until his death in 2005.

To make the most of the day, arrive at the *duomo* very early. The feast day is a national media event and brings out both celebrities and local dignitaries. A group of women called the *parenti de San Gennaro* accompany the ritual with prayers until the liquefaction is signalled by a white handkerchief.

You probably won't see the actual event close up due to the overwhelming crowds, but the visual chaos and religious splendour is sure to fascinate.

⏶ *The* duomo – *tranquil here – is filled to bursting point at San Gennaro*

History

Naples has been an important trading post ever since it was founded by the Greeks in the 5th century BC. The Greeks were attracted by the lush soils of the region. Unfortunately, it was volcanic activity that gave the soil its nutrients.

By the 3rd century, Naples had been absorbed into the Roman Empire. While the region became a much-favoured playground for the rich, its status as a trade centre declined as locals were forced to build ships and supply men for the Roman navy. The eruption of Vesuvius in AD 79 was deadly, but economic depression had driven many residents away by this point. Had the volcano erupted a mere century earlier, thousands more inhabitants would have perished.

In AD 645, the tight rein of the Empire loosened. For the first time in centuries, home rule was given to a local duke and the city flourished. Attracted by booming trade and a flourishing arts scene, foreign invaders attacked relentlessly. Naples finally surrendered to the Norman King Roger and was absorbed into the Kingdom of Sicily in 1077. Trade once again declined and the city re-entered a period of economic depression.

Norman decline ushered in the rule of Charles of Anjou in 1256. To set him apart from his predecessors, Anjou moved the capital of the Kingdom from Palermo to Naples and the city entered yet another boom period. But this period of French reign was brief, with control eventually given to the Aragonese in 1302.

For two centuries, the Aragonese ruled over a unified Southern Italy until the departure of Ferdinand III in 1502. Viceroys, despised by the local population, continued to rule in their absence for the

Historical relief at Castel Nuovo

next 250 years. Despite the hated leadership, Naples became Europe's largest city with a population of 300,000 in 1600.

Between 1631 and 1656, plague and an eruption of Vesuvius killed three-quarters of the population. Following this period of destruction, residents began to rebuild in the baroque style. Many of the churches visible today can be traced back to the mid-17th century.

The Aragonese and Habsburgs continued to rule over Naples until 1860 when the region joined a unified Italy. Cholera outbreaks and mass emigration to North America depleted the population, but it was World War II that truly damaged the city's heart. Mass bombing of the ports and German destruction of the city's infrastructure forced one-third of the female population into prostitution and gave power to the *camorra* mafia clans.

Today, corruption clean-up campaigns, a new metro system and a blossoming IT industry have combined to give the city back its soul. It may never again be the world's economic powerhouse, but its citizens probably wouldn't want that kind of responsibility.

Lifestyle

The citizens of Naples are the most laid-back in Italy. Definitely of a 'work-to-live' mindset, they adore a good party – be it religious, cultural or just a family get-together. This relaxed attitude to life has caused other Italians to view Neapolitans as something akin to a lazy cousin – always a lot of fun but never all that motivated. But in recent years things have changed.

● *Definitely the best way to get around town*

Since the early 90s, Naples has experienced a bit of a boom. Most trace Naples' newfound fortunes back to 1994 when the city was spruced up to host a G7 summit. A new metro system is doing much to create sparks in the business community as the region's epic traffic problems are finally being addressed. What's more, a blossoming IT industry is beginning to take shape.

The Circumvesuviana railway serves as a lifeline for the region, shuttling commuters up and down the coast between Naples, Pompeii, Herculaneum, Sorrento and all points in-between. The Campanian coastline served by the railway is a mix of historic landmarks squeezed between some of Europe's most densely populated towns.

This crush of people perhaps explains Neapolitan body language. Need to get a point across? Residents will have the precise finger wave, point, shrug or slouch to do it.

The famed *camorra* mafia clans that gave Naples its crime-filled reputation are largely a thing of the past. There are still black-market dealings involving unions and black-market cigarette sales, but tourists probably won't see or experience anything.

Formerly a no-go area, the waterfront has been cleaned up and a Sunday afternoon stroll along the coast is popular with families. After dark, things can get a bit dodgy so keep valuables at home. Courting couples especially love watching the sunset from the well-placed benches.

To do as the locals do, head to any of the numerous piazzas that are dotted throughout the city. **Piazza Bellini** is a particular favourite. After dark, these public squares become hives of activity filled with chattering friends, performers, musicians, and Vespa-travelling youngsters all on the lookout for their next boy/girlfriend.

Culture

Before the clean-up campaign of the mid-90s, the bulk of Neapolitan art could be found inside churches or under a layer of dust at the **Museo di Capodimonte**. A resurgence in local pride has changed all that, as a boom in street and modern art has injected vibrancy into the local cultural scene. The local government is committed to funding public art, with intriguing displays viewable at almost every metro station.

● *The sumptuous interior of the Teatro San Carlo*

Art lovers will rejoice in the possibility of examining gilded Baroque treasures in the churches of Centro Storico by day, and large-scale cutting-edge outdoor installations in the Piazza del Plebiscito as the sun sets.

Exhibition spaces at the Castel Sant'Elmo and Museo Nazionale Archeologico have attracted some of the biggest names in the art world, including Jeff Koons, Francesco Clemente and Damien Hirst. And let's not forget the incredible works of Roman art rescued from Pompeii, on show both at the Museo Nazionale Archeologico and on the site itself.

If you're in the market to make a purchase, Alfonso Artiaco, Studio Trisorio and Raucci Santamaria tend to offer the most innovative and exciting exhibitions of new work.

Alfonso Artiaco ⓐ Piazza dei Martiri 58 ① 081 497 6072
ⓦ www.alfonsoartiaco.com
Castel Sant'Elmo ⓐ Via Tito Angelini 22 ① 081 578 4030
Museo Nazionale Archeologico ⓐ Piazza Museo 19 ① 081 564 8941
ⓦ www.archeona.arti.beniculturali.it
Raucci Santamaria ⓐ Corso Amedeo di Savoia 190 ① 081 744 3645
Studio Trisorio ⓐ Riviera di Chiaia 215 ① 081 414 306
ⓦ www.studiotrisorio.com

CINEMA

As the hometown of Sophia Loren, Naples especially loves a night at the cinema. Don't go if you are expecting a quiet night; the movies are considered a social occasion complete with all the chattering and phone ringing that might entail. Film buffs may go slowly insane as the evening progresses. In warm weather, free films are often shown at the Centro Direzionale, in the

WWF reserve at Astroni and at the Castel Nuovo. Check listings for showtimes.

Academy Astra ⓐ Via Mezzocanone 109 ❶ 081 552 0713
Modernissimo ⓐ Via Cisterna dell'Olio 59 ❶ 081 551 1247
Warner Village Metropolitan Napoli ⓐ Via Chiaia 149 ❶ 081 252 5133
ⓦ www.warnervillage.it

THE STAGE

For theatre and opera, look no further than the **Teatro San Carlo**. Originally constructed in 1737, the current building is actually a replacement built in 1816 following a fire. Standards are exceptional – second only to Milan's La Scala – and tickets are justifiably hard to come by. Repertoires rely mainly on traditional classics.

Teatro San Carlo ⓐ Via San Carlo 98F ❶ 081 797 2331
ⓦ www.teatrosancarlo.it

OUTSIDE ENTERTAINMENT

The Neapolitan love affair with warm weather is enhanced in the summer when outdoor music festivals bring first-class performances. The most famous celebration is the Festival Musicale di Villa Rufolo, which runs from June to August. Some of the performances are staged in a 12th-century villa in Ravello where Wagner composed sections of *Parsifal*.

Festival Musicale di Villa Rufolo ⓐ Via Trinità 3, Ravello ❶ 089 858 149 ⓦ www.ravelloarts.org

❶ *The imposing Castel dell'Ovo*

Shopping

Unlike some of its more fashionable neighbours to the north, Naples isn't considered a shopping town. Until recently many residents couldn't afford luxury goods. All of this is changing as the economy continues to improve.

The big designer labels (Gucci, Armani, Ferragamo, Valentino) have stand-alone shops on the streets in and around Piazza dei Martiri in Chiaia. Don't expect entire collections. For that you'll need to head to Milan or Rome. But designer goods aren't the best buy in this bargain-loving town.

Neapolitans are social creatures, and shopping is considered a social event. Markets provide the widest selection, intriguing buys and most colourful displays in this town, selling everything from high-quality leather shoes to knock-off mobile phones.

USEFUL SHOPPING PHRASES

What time do the shops open/close?
A che ora aprono/chiudono i negozi?
Ah keh awra ahprawnaw/kewdawnaw ee nehgotsee?

How much is this?	**Can I try this on?**
Quant' è?	Posso provarlo?
Kwahnteh?	*Pawssaw prawvarrlaw?*

My size is ...	**I'll take this one, thank you**
La mia taglia è ...	Prenderò questo, grazie
Lah meeyah tahlyah eh ...	*Prehndehroh kwestaw, grahtsyeh*

The biggest market is **La Pignassecca**, located on the streets in and around Piazzetta Montesanto. Be sure to go early and remember to take cash as most stalls don't take credit/debit cards.

For something less expensive than designer labels yet more salubrious than the market stalls, follow the middle classes to **Galleria Umberto** and up via Toledo. The Galleria is a wonderfully atmospheric covered shopping centre in need of some TLC but which provides a bit of Italian flair and drama. The via Toledo, meanwhile, is like the Oxford Street or Fifth Avenue of Naples. Branches of high street favourites and Italian department stores can be found along this stretch. Avoid the via Toledo on Saturday evenings between 18.00 and 20.00 as the crowds can be overwhelming and pickpocketing becomes a major problem.

Food and drink are the best buys in Naples, thanks to the region's culinary traditions. Almost every tourist picks up a bottle of the city's favourite alcoholic tipple, limoncello. For the best stuff, wait until you hit Capri, as this is where the drink was originally distilled.

⬢ *Top shopping in the Galleria Umberto*

Eating & drinking

Neapolitans love their food. Naples is the home of pizza, but that's not all there is to enjoy. Fresh seafood, locally produced wine, sun-ripened produce and the sweetest ice cream you've ever tasted are just some of the treats in store.

Ethnic cuisine isn't really an option. Italian food, like mama used to make, is what you'll find lining the streets of Naples – which means that meals are filling, generous and made with love.

> **RESTAURANT CATEGORIES**
> Price ratings in this book are based on a three-course meal without drinks: **£ up to €10; ££ between €10 and €20; £££ above €20**

🔺 *Neapolitan pizza – the best in the world*

EATING

Food is an important feature in the daily life of a typical Neapolitan. Most establishments are family run and have been patronised loyally by the same clientele for years, if not generations. For them, it's the tastebuds rather than the décor that matters, so don't be surprised if some of your best meals are in the dingiest of cafés.

- Restaurant hours vary wildly, so always check ahead.
- If an eatery opens for **lunch** – although many of them don't – then opening hours will be between 12.00 and 15.00. On Thursdays and Fridays the establishment may stay open for an extra hour until 16.00, but this isn't always the case.
- For **dinner**, restaurants will usually open between 19.00 and 19.30. They can close any time between 22.00 and 24.00 depending on the evening, the size of the crowd, whether there is an opera premiere at San Carlo and/or if it happens to be raining.
- Occasionally, restaurants will shut if there's an important football match on television.
- Most establishments also shut on a Sunday evening and one whole day in the week – usually Monday or Tuesday.

MENUS

When choosing your dish, it is best to avoid ordering from the *menu turistico* as most items will have been prepared earlier in the week and frozen. Instead, opt for the *menu del giorno*. Be adventurous. Some of Naples' best eateries are in the most unlikely of locations. Restaurants near tourist hotspots may look popular, but that's usually due to convenience rather than any culinary 'wow' factor.

Many menus may be written in local dialect or feature a dish that is a speciality of the establishment. When in doubt, take a look at what other diners are tucking into and point.

Vegetarians shouldn't encounter difficulties with eating in Naples. There are always plenty of pasta dishes, pizzas and tomato-based sauces to choose from. Be aware, though, that southern Italians don't think of ham or bacon as meat. So, if you're uncertain about a dish, it's always a good idea to ask: *'C'è la pancetta?'* ('Is there bacon in it?')

Naples is thought to be the traditional home of the pizza and credits itself as having given birth to the first slice in the 16th century. This legend has resulted in the simple pizza pie being elevated to an art form. There are thousands of *pizzerias* throughout the city. Despite this, locals each have their favourite pizza and will debate endlessly on its individual merits.

● *A sunny spot and a slice of pizza*

A good pizza should have a soft, thin base, medium amounts of topping surrounded by a thick doughy rim. It should be baked in a wood-fuelled fire. The most popular establishments will always have a long queue snaking from the door. Don't let this put you off; queues tend to move fast!

Italians generally enjoy a glass of wine with their meal. House wines are invariably local and generally very good. Between April and November, red wine is a better option as the current year's production becomes available.

If you enjoy a cup of coffee after your meal, be aware that many restaurants serve only *espresso*. If this doesn't sit well with you, try weaning yourself off caffeine with a shot of traditional *digestive*: limoncello, nocillo (made with hazelnuts) or basilica (basil).

USEFUL DINING PHRASES

I would like a table for ... people.
Vorrei un tavolo per ... persone.
Vawrray oon tahvawlaw perr ... perrsawneh.

Waiter/waitress!	**May I have the bill, please?**
Cameriere/cameriera!	Mi dà il conto, per favore.
Cahmehryereh/cahmehryera!	*Mee dah eel cawntaw, perr fahvawreh.*

I am a vegetarian. Does this contain meat?
Sono vegetariano/vegetariana (fem.). Contiene carne?
Sawnaw vejetahreeahnaw/vejetahreeahnah.
Contyehneh kahrneh?

Entertainment & nightlife

During the early 20th century, Naples had a reputation as a centre for Italian music. For many visitors, *in canzone napoletano* (popular songs) continue to define the nation. 'O Surdato Annamurato' and 'Funiculì, Funiculà' are all-time favourites of this genre – but they're hardly what you might call cutting edge.

The music and nightlife of Naples occurs on the street. As population density is so high in this city, music venues are painfully small. Promoters, therefore, can't attract big-name acts as sell-outs wouldn't even begin to cover their appearance fees. Instead, a good rockin' night out will require hunting for local bands, such as 24 Grana, La Notte della Taranta (featuring ex-Police drummer Stewart Copeland), Pino Daniele and acclaimed jazz saxophonist Daniele Sepe. If you are lucky, you may even see Sepe perform on the street.

The biggest venue in Naples is Palapartenope. While it's absolutely soulless, it does occasionally bring in interesting acts and should be your first stop if live music is on your list of things to do.

Palapartenope ❸ Via Barbagallo 15 ❶ 081 570 0008
Ⓦ www.palapartenope.it

Naples is very much a neighbourhood town with different 'types' of people attracted to individual areas. After dark, the waterfront of Chiaia and Mergellina is very traditional. Families, the older generation and suburbanites love spending a weekend evening strolling along the bay, eating ice cream, drinking a limoncello (or two) and catching up on gossip.

Meanwhile, Centro Storico is geared towards artists, intellectuals and students. These younger crowds enjoying living *La vie Bohème*:

⏵ *Try a night at the opera at the Teatro San Carlo*

they hang out on the steps and in public squares – particularly on Piazza San Domenico Maggiore, Piazza del Gesù, via Cisterna dell'Olio and (especially) Piazza Bellini.

During the summer, the heat makes it almost impossible to go inside any of the venues in the Centro Storico. Instead, grab a beer and walk around the streets until you find a congenial group of locals to join. This doesn't usually take long.

Locals, both young and old, generally leave their homes late when embarking on a night on the town. Eleven o'clock (23.00) is the earliest you should even consider leaving your hotel. Midnight is even better. If you are really desperate to get inside a particular club and/or bar, then go when the doors open, but be prepared to be the only ones in the place for a long while.

Clubbing and pubbing not your thing? Don't worry. Neapolitans are huge fans of the classics, particularly opera. The Teatro San Carlo is rated as second only to La Scala (Milan) in terms of prestige.

BARS & CLUBS

ⓘ Getting into clubs can involve much bartering and negotiation. Bars and nightclubs are generally the size of a postage stamp and admittance numbers are very limited.

- A membership card, which will cost a fee, is sometimes required.
- A door fee, which sometimes includes the cost of one drink, will also be charged.
- If you are given a card when you enter a venue, you will need to get it stamped every time you get a drink, as this is how the bar charges you at the end of the evening. Lose it and you will be subjected to a hefty fine.

Performances are top-notch (if a little staid) and sell out well in advance. If you want to see anything, purchase your ticket before arriving in the city or be prepared to spend a small fortune with one of the ticket hawkers outside. ❶ Be warned: many of the tickets sold by hawkers are forgeries or invalid.

Teatro San Carlo ➋ Via San Carlo 98F ❶ 081 797 2331 ⓦ www.teatrosancarlo.it

🔺 *Heading for a good night out in Chiaia*

Sport & relaxation

Neapolitans live and die by sport. Whether watching or playing, they put their heart and soul into it (and make sure they look good while doing so). Football rules the roost, with locals devoted to the success or failure of their home team SS CalcioNapoli. While the days of championships and Maradona are over, matches are still exciting affairs. Tickets are like gold dust but can usually be picked up from ticket sellers outside the stadium on match days. It's also worth trying the Azzuro Service box office; you never know when a pair of seats becomes available.

Azzuro Service ⓐ Via F Galeoata 17 ⓣ 081 593 4001
ⓦ www.azzurroservice.it

As Naples is situated on the coast, it should be no surprise that fishing and swimming are popular recreational activities. The water in Naples proper is far from clean. But you don't have to go too far to find areas suitable for a dip.

The best locations for a day's swimming are the rocky and pebbly coves on the outlying islands of Capri, Procida and Ischia. Sorrento and the Amalfi Coast also have comfortable nooks where you can enjoy a dip and a spot of sunbathing. Boats based in these cleaner ports are also well-placed and priced for a fishing excursion. So if you want to enjoy the sea, it's best to leave town.

If this proves inconvenient or impossible during your stay, then head in the direction of Mergellina where there are a few spots safe enough to risk.

To keep fit, follow the locals to the various green spaces scattered throughout town. Jogging is extremely popular among fit Neapolitans, with Parco Virginiano and Bosco di Capodimonte often clogged with trainer-clad enthusiasts on weekend mornings.

A more romantic suggestion is to row your way around the bay at sunset. Not only do you get a great workout, but also you'll enjoy some of the best views of Naples. Boat rentals can be arranged just off the bridge leading to the Castel dell'Ovo.

⬥ *Football is almost a religion in Naples*

Accommodation

Naples is probably the only city in Italy that doesn't have a 5-star hotel. This isn't due to lack of quality; it's because Italy's strange rating system is focused around amenities rather than history, ambience or service.

For what you get, Neapolitan hotels tend to be overpriced. Summertime can bring occasional weekday deals in the city as locals flee for cooler climes. The exception to this rule is in the sea-facing hotels that line the via Partenope.

You'll need a bargain during your stay in Naples if you are even remotely thinking of hitting the more popular summer resorts of Ischia, Capri or the Amalfi Coast. Room rates here can soar into the stratosphere with 3-star properties starting at €300 per night.

Development, investment and a boom in inbound tourism due to many new low-cost flights have transformed the accommodation scene in Naples. A decade ago, the only options were crumbling 'grand dame' hotels or flea-pits close to the railway station. Today there are boutique hotels with designer accoutrements, converted *palazzos* and B&Bs oozing with character. Hotel developments are constantly being talked about, so when planning your trip keep your eyes peeled in travel news pages to see when openings occur.

PRICE RATINGS

Hotels in Italy are graded according to a star system (1 star for a cheap pensione to 5 stars for a luxurious resort with numerous facilities). Ratings in this book are for a single night in a double room/two persons.

£ up to €80; ££ €80–€140; £££ over €140

HOTELS & GUEST HOUSES

Canada £ In town for just one night before hopping over to the islands? Then stay at the Canada. Located just seconds from the Mergellina hydrofoil port, it's the perfect place to rest your head if a quick transfer is what you're after. ⓐ Via Mergellina 43 ⓣ 081 680 952 ⓦ www.sea-hotels.com

Hotel des Artistes £ Live in the Bohemian quarter in this traditionally kitted out property close to all the main sights of the Centro Storico. For such a central location, rooms are surprisingly quiet. ⓐ Via del Duomo 61 ⓣ 081 446 155 ⓦ www.hoteldesartistesnaples.it

La Fontane al Mare £ Guests at this property choose it as it's one of the most affordable places in Naples located along the seafront. It may not be chic, but the small terrace provides memorable views. ⓐ Via N Tommaseo 14 ⓣ 081 764 3811

Il Convento £–££ This converted 15th-century convent boasts a central location just off the via Toledo, wood-beamed ceilings and a rustic, yet comfortable charm. ⓐ Via Speranzella 137/A ⓣ 081 403 977 ⓦ www.hotelilconvento.com

Britannique ££ Originally built to cash in on the wave of British tourists embarking on grand tours during the 19th century, this private villa still brings in the Brits due to its combination of colonial era charm and elegance. ⓐ Corso Vittorio Emanuele 133 ⓣ 081 761 4145

Caravaggio Hotel di Napoli ££ This property was one of the first to be restored from dilapidated villa to chic boutique hotel. Outside is a stunning 17th-century exterior; inside is all modern light and air. ● Piazza Cardinale Sisto Riario Sforza 157 ● 081 211 0066 ● www.caravaggiohotel.it

Chiaia Hotel de Charme ££ Old-fashioned class combines with modern convenience. This newly restored property is just seconds from the Palazzo Reale. Some of the rooms even have Jacuzzis. ● Via Chiaia 216 ● 081 415 555 ● www.hotelchiaia.it

Parteno ££ If sea views and a via Partenope address are what you want, but your budget doesn't agree, choose this cosy, personal hotel filled with charming individual touches. ● Via Partenope 1 ● 081 245 2095 ● www.parteno.it

Excelsior £££ Politicians, jet-setters, celebrities and A-listers choose the Excelsior as their address of choice when they're in town. Each room is unique and worth the investment. ● Via Partenope 48 ● 081 764 0111 ● www.excelsior.it

Grand Hotel Parker's £££ Staying in this luxurious 5-star hotel is like returning to the 19th century when the hotel was the base for travellers embarking on a traditional European 'grand tour'. A recent restoration has returned it to its original splendour. ● Corso Vittorio Emanuele 135 ● 081 761 2474 ● www.grandhotelparkers.com

● *Chic boutique hotel Caravaggio*

Miramare £££ This converted art deco villa dating back to 1914 continues to attract celebrities and starlets, drawn by the breathtaking views over the bay. ⓐ Via Nazario Sauro 24 ① 081 764 7589 ⓦ www.hotelmiramare.com

Vesuvio £££ Another celebrity favourite on the Santa Lucia seafront. The luxury here has attracted everyone from Queen Victoria to Bill Clinton. An outdoor swimming pool will join the hotel's long list of amenities some time in 2007. ⓐ Via Partenope 45 ① 081 764 0044 ⓦ www.vesuvio.it

🔺 *The elegant and upmarket Hotel Excelsior*

Villa Capodimonte £££ Looking for somewhere quiet? Then this gorgeous villa on Capodimonte hill should fit the bill. The views of the bay from the private terraces are spectacular. **ⓐ** Via Moiariello 66 **ⓣ** 081 459 0000 **ⓦ** www.villacapodimonte.it

HOSTELS & CAMPSITES

Agriturismo Il Casolare di Tobia £ This 19th-century farmhouse is situated in an extinct volcanic crater surrounded by vineyards. While it's far from town, the gardens and views over the fields more than make up for the transport inconvenience. **ⓐ** Contrada Coste di Baia, Via Selvatico 12, Bacoli **ⓣ** 081 523 5193 **ⓦ** www.datobia.it

Averno £ This campsite is perfect if your priority is sun and fun. Situated in the Campi Flegrei, it's some distance from Naples but just 2 km (1 mile) to the beach. **ⓐ** Via Montenuovo Licola Patria 85, Arco Felice Lucrino, Pozzuoli **ⓣ** 081 804 2666 **ⓦ** www.averno.it

Ostello Mergellina £ Clean, airy rooms with light wood furniture make this hostel a popular option with backpackers. Guests can book either private double rooms or dormitory beds. Booking for space in July or August is a must. **ⓐ** Salita della Grotta a Piedigrotta 23 **ⓣ** 081 761 1215

Vulcano Solfatara £ This campsite is the most conveniently located site for visiting Naples. Just 800 m (about ½ mile) from the Pozzuoli metro stop, it's a popular place for travellers on a budget. Bungalows are also available to rent if you can't bear to stay one more night in a tent. **ⓐ** Via Solfatara 161 **ⓣ** 081 526 7413 **ⓦ** www.solfatara.it

THE BEST OF NAPLES

Naples is an ideal destination for a short weekend break, because most of the main attractions are grouped together in either the Centro Storico or Royal Naples neighbourhoods. For day-trip suggestions, see pages 42–3.

TOP 10 ATTRACTIONS

- **Palazzo Reale** Home to the Bourbon monarchs for almost three centuries, this *palazzo* is truly stunning (see page 61).

- **The Piazzetta in Capri** People-watching at its finest. Everybody who is anybody eventually passes through this tiny square with four cafés fighting for your patronage (see page 129).

- **Positano** The view of this pastel-toned town spilling down steep cliffs and rocks towards the sea is breathtaking (see page 119).

- **Pompeii** Seeing the once-buried Roman town became a must-stop on any discerning traveller's 'grand tour' itinerary – a fact that remains to this day (see page 105).

- **Teatro San Carlo** Second only to Milan's La Scala, this jewel-box of an opera house draws in the big names (see page 20).

- **Duomo** Naples' cathedral houses the remains of its patron saint, San Gennaro. The feast day is a spectacle of prayer, wailing and miracles (see page 12).

- **Museo Nazionale Archeologico** If you've been wondering where they put all the artefacts dug from the sites at Pompeii and Herculaneum, then look no further (see page 19).

- **Castel Sant'Elmo** This atmospheric castle has stood here since 1329. Go during one of the frequent art exhibitions when visitors are permitted to walk through the eerie interiors (see page 88).

- **Pizza and limoncello** As the hometown of pizza, you'll never go wrong with a slice – and limoncello is the local contribution to the drinks cabinet (see pages 26–7).

- **La Pignassecca** See how locals live with a visit to this massive market selling everything from leather and lace to lettuce and laxatives (see page 23).

🔽 *Castel Nuovo*

Here is a brief guide to seeing and experiencing the best of Naples, depending on the time you have available.

HALF-DAY: NAPLES IN A HURRY

Stick close to the Centro Storico and Royal Naples neighbourhoods by starting your journey in the Piazza del Plebiscito. Pop into the

🔺 *Take time to visit the Museo di Capodimonte*

Palazzo Reale to enjoy the pomp and pageantry followed by a quick coffee at Caffè Gambrinus. From here, you can window shop as you pass through the covered arcades of the Galleria Umberto or head directly to the via Toledo.

Quick stops inside the Gesù Nuovo and Santa Chiara churches will expose you to a little bit of Centro Storico religion and neighbourhood culture before ending the day at the Museo Nazionale Archeologico. If time is of the essence, head straight for the Pompeii exhibitions on the top floor.

1 DAY: TIME TO SEE A LITTLE MORE

If you can spare the other half of the day, then explore the Centro Storico more fully, making sure you add the *duomo* to the list. Top off the day by sipping a drink at any of the cafés on the Piazza Bellini – preferably after 24.00 when local bohemians and the student population come out to play.

2–3 DAYS: SHORT CITY-BREAK

Two or three days will give you a much better impression of what the city has to offer. As well as the suggestions above, make side trips on a funicular up to Vomero and the Castel Nuovo. Alternatively, take a trip to the art collections and jogging trails of the Museo di Capodimonte. A journey out of town on the Circumvesuviana railway to Pompeii should also be factored in.

LONGER: ENJOYING NAPLES TO THE FULL

Get more out of Naples by getting out of town. A drive along the Amalfi Coast or a ferry journey to Capri or Ischia will expose you to a different side of Campanian culture and provide many lasting memories.

Something for nothing

It's easy to spend buckets of cash in a city like Naples, but with a little bit of planning, your stay need not be expensive. The very fact that the city's main attractions are located within a compact area means you can often dispense with public transport and walk. As the city enjoys a Mediterranean climate, a stroll along the waterfront is an enjoyable way to spend an hour or two, especially if there are public performances in the grandstand of the Villa Comunale.

There is a religious festival of some sort almost every weekend. Many of these celebrations are extremely local events. Don't let this dissuade you! You'll be made to feel most welcome if you join in. Thrifty culture freaks should make sure they are in town during *Settimana per la cultura* – a single week in April when all the museums are open to the public free of charge.

The cheapest thing to do that will expose you to 'real' Naples is a visit to the city's churches. While some of the bigger places of worship charge an admission fee, most do not – and there are literally hundreds of churches to wander through.

Not exactly free, a ride on the funicular up to Vomero is well worth the €1 expense. Not only has this inspired a famed Neapolitan song, but also it takes you up to one of the most serene districts of town. The views from the top over the Centro Storico and bay should be more than enough to reassure you.

After dark, you don't need to spend a fortune to have a good time. For something more traditional, the street-side activity along the Chiaia waterfront brings out families, black-clad grandmothers and gaggles of young couples from the suburbs. Purchase a *gelato* (ice cream) and you'll be set for the evening.

Alternatively, hang with the hipsters in the Piazza Bellini where, for the cost of an espresso, you can debate politics, admire buskers or make eyes at one of the locals as they try to seduce you from the back of their Vespas.

◆ *Take a free dip at one of Naples' public beaches*

When it rains

The occasional shower should not equal disaster during your stay in Naples. There are more than enough churches and museums to take shelter in. If the storm looks like it's going to be prolonged, head to one of the bigger sights. The Museo Nazionale, Duomo, Palazzo

⬤ *Keep out of the rain in the catacombs of San Gennaro (see page 91)*

Reale or Museo di Capodimonte are the obvious possibilities. Each is big enough to keep you occupied for at least two hours.

Shopaholics will appreciate the covered arcades of the Galleria Umberto. Some of the shops can be quite chic, featuring the finest Italian fashions. Other boutiques are filled with overpriced tat. There are panes of glass missing from the ceiling, meaning that the floor can be covered in slick water, so be sure to watch your step.

Combine architectural history with an attack on your budget by visiting the local branch of the nationwide department store La Rinascente. Located in a converted *palazzo* on the via Toledo, it's a beautiful emporium. Too bad the wares are a bit pedestrian.

In the evenings, options do become limited, especially during the summer. Go inside and you face a wilt-inducing wall of humidity. Stay outside and you'll get drenched. Neapolitans often choose rainy nights to go to the movies where air conditioning and gossiping await. You should also consider this option, but only if you speak Italian. Subtitles are rare and most English films are dubbed into the local lingo.

If the Amalfi Coast or Pompeii are in your plans, think twice about visiting during a grey-weather day. The stretch of road along the Amalfi Coast is extremely treacherous even on dry days. When rain hits the pavement, it can become a death trap. Pompeii and Herculaneum are also no-go areas, as there is absolutely no cover anywhere on either site. Pompeii, especially, is best avoided as the streets can be extremely muddy.

The ferries and hydrofoils maintain their schedules no matter what the weather has in store. Cancellations do occur, but the storms have to be extremely strong to warrant it. Hydrofoils are much more prone to cancellation than ferries so if you absolutely have to get to your final destination, choose the slower surer ferryboats.

On arrival

Most travellers visiting Naples will arrive by plane at Capodichino Airport. The airport is very close to town, located just 8 km (5 miles) from the centre.

🛈 If you arrive during the traditional rush hours you are likely to face heavy traffic.

TIME DIFFERENCES

Italian clocks follow Central European Time (CET). During Daylight Saving Time (end Mar–end Oct), the clocks are put ahead 1 hour. In the Italian summer, at 12.00 noon, the time elsewhere is as follows:

Australia Eastern Standard Time 20.00, Central Standard Time 19.30, Western Standard Time 18.00
New Zealand 22.00
South Africa 12.00
UK and Republic of Ireland 11.00
US and Canada Newfoundland Time 07.30, Atlantic Canada Time 07.00, Eastern Standard Time 06.00, Central Time 05.00, Mountain Time 04.00, Pacific Time 03.00, Alaska 02.00

ARRIVING

By air

Naples International Airport, otherwise known as the Aeroporto Internazionale di Napoli (Capodichino) is 8 km (5 miles) from the centre of town. While it is southern Italy's largest airport, it isn't packed with facilities. Short-haul traffic makes up the bulk of flights, with the occasional charter servicing longer-haul destinations.

Getting to town is very easy. The journey to Stazione Centrale railway station takes 5 to 10 minutes and 20 minutes to the ferry and hydrofoil ports. If you're on a budget, direct bus services make the trip to both destinations throughout the day. Alibus (☎ 800 639 525) is the most recommended private bus service. It departs every 30 minutes from just outside the arrivals level to the Piazza Garibaldi exit of the Stazione Central and Piazza Municipio near the main port. Buses run from 05.55 to 23.55 and cost €3 each way.

Local buses are also a possibility. Look for the orange route 3S bus that departs every 15 minutes from outside the arrivals lounge. Tickets need to be purchased in advance from the *tabacchi* inside the airport and cost €1 each way. This method should only be considered if you pack light, as pickpockets are common. Don't forget to stamp your ticket once you board.

Hailing a taxi isn't a problem as there are usually dozens waiting for customers. Depending on traffic, the trip should cost between €15 and €20.

By rail

There are three mainline stations in Naples. The one most foreign travellers arrive at is the Stazione Centrale in Piazza Garibaldi. All rapid services such as Eurostar and Intercity use this station.

Below street level are two lower levels. The first lower level houses the ticket counter for the Circumvesuviana line servicing Pompeii, Herculaneum and all points to Sorrento. The second level down is Piazza Garibaldi station used by suburban and local metro lines.

Some services also stop at Naples' other two mainline stations: Mergellina and Campi Flegrei. Check with your hotel to see if either of these stations are closer to your final destination.

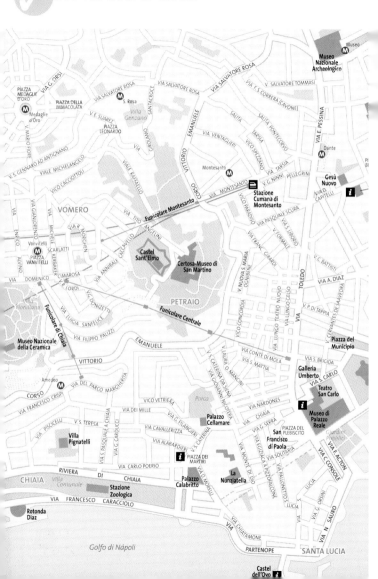

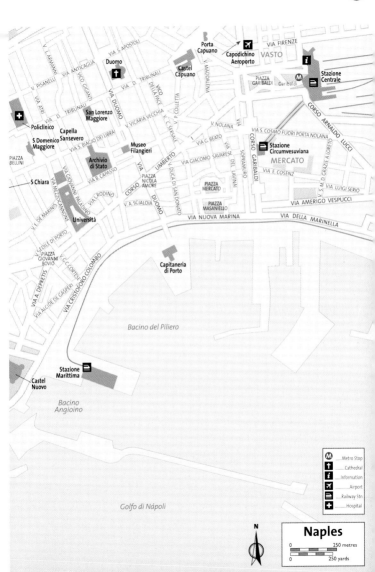

Naples

By road

Think twice before deciding to drive to Naples. While you will need a car if you are planning a drive along the Amalfi Coast, car theft is rife, parking is impossible and city traffic is legendarily awful.

If you must bring your car, the easiest way to get here is by using Italy's motorways. From Rome and points north, take the A1 south and follow the signs to Naples. From the south and the Sorrentine Peninsula, it's the A3 motorway that will get you to your final destination.

By boat

More and more cruise ships are including Naples on their itineraries. If you are visiting as part of a cruise, the chances are your first sighting of the city will be at the Molo Beverello. While not the most picturesque of corners, it's just a few steps away from the Palazzo Reale. Just cross the street and turn left!

FINDING YOUR FEET

Because central Naples is relatively compact, it doesn't take long to get the hang of the place. While pedestrian zones are few, the size of the streets in the Centro Storico force many to walk on the cobbles. Just watch out for flying Vespas! Naples may have a bad crime reputation, but this is largely unjustified. Various clean-up campaigns conducted through the 90s have turned the statistics around. Piazza Garibaldi, the neighbourhood surrounding the railway station and the port district can be a bit dodgy, so it is best to keep valuables hidden or back at your hotel.

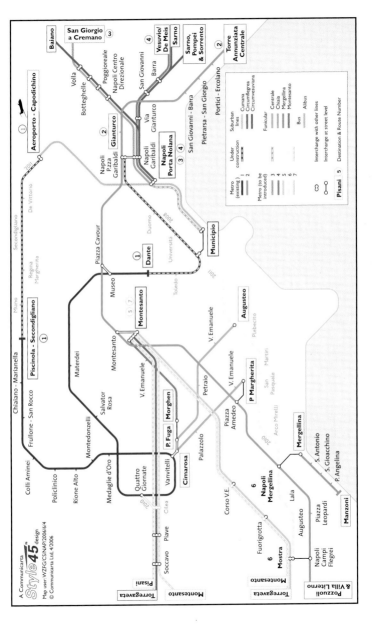

ORIENTATION

The streets of Naples are maze-like. The easiest way to navigate is to use the Piazza del Plebiscito as a base and get your bearings from there. At the south of the piazza, turn right and follow the street to the fishermen's quarter of Santa Lucia. Keep going farther to reach the chic shops of Chiaia.

To the north of the piazza is the via Toledo, considered to be the Oxford Street or Fifth Avenue of the city. Formerly home to the rich and elite, their *palazzos* now house department stores and cafés. Keep going far enough on the via Toledo and you'll reach the Museo Nazionale Archeologico. Lying even farther north and on the top of a hill is Capodimonte. You'll need to make a bus or car journey to reach the museum that lies at the heart of this district.

IF YOU GET LOST, TRY ...

Excuse me, do you speak English?
Mi scusi, parla inglese?
Mee scoozee, parrla eenglehzeh?

Excuse me, is this the right way to the old town/the city centre/the tourist office/ the station/the bus station?
Mi scusi, è questa la strada per città vecchia/al centro città/l'ufficio informazioni turistiche/alla stazione ferroviaria/ alla stazione degli autobus?
Mee scoozee, eh kwehstah lah strahda perr lah cheetta vehkyah/ahl chentraw cheetteh/looffeechaw eenforrmahtsyawnee tooreesteekeh/ahlla stahtsyawneh ferrawvyarya/ahlla stahtsyawneh delee ahootawboos?

TRAVELLING BY BUS

❶ Bus tickets must be purchased in advance. You can get them from *tabacchi* at a cost of €1 each. Once you board the bus, don't forget to get the ticket stamped. The ticket will then be valid for 90 minutes. Metro and funicular tickets also cost €1 each, but can be purchased at the station.

From the via Toledo, a quick turn right will lead you into the winding streets of the Centro Storico; to the left is the Funicolare Centrale leading up to Vomero and the Castel Nuovo.

Finally, pass through the Palazzo Reale from the Piazza del Plebiscito to reach the Piazza Municipio. From here, go up the via Depretis to Corso Umberto I. This road will lead you to the Piazza Garibaldi and the Stazione Centrale. ▲

GETTING AROUND

Naples used to be difficult to get around by public transport. However, the new metro system means this is no longer a problem. While the lines may not take you everywhere you want to go, they will do shortly as new lines open. The bus system is more extensive, but the volume of traffic often means it will take you longer to get to your destination than it would have if you'd walked.

⬤ *M for metro*

Car hire

Unless you are planning an Amalfi Coast drive, don't hire a car. It won't get you anywhere fast, you won't be able to park it and you'll probably get it scratched. For truly fast access, consider renting a scooter.

❶ The minimum age for renting an economy car is 21 (25 for a larger one). Make sure you're covered for both theft and collision damage.

Local and international rental companies include:

Avis ❶ 199 100 133 Ⓦ www.avisautonoleggio.it
Europcar ❶ 800 014 410 Ⓦ www.europcar.it
Hertz ❶ 081 780 2971 Ⓦ www.hertz.it
Maggiore-Budget ❶ 848 867 067 Ⓦ www.maggiore.it
Thrifty ❶ 081 780 5702 Ⓦ www.italybycar.it

🔽 *Save your legs and take the funicular*

▶ *View of the city from Vomero*

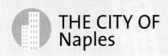

Royal Naples & Chiaia

The Royal Naples district has been the site of Neapolitan power ever since the city was founded over 2,500 years ago. Here is where you will find the winding streets of Pallonetto's rambling fishermen's quarters, the Palazzo Reale and the military might of the Castel dell'Ovo.

Visitors interested in exploring the royal connections of the city and its history as a major Mediterranean superpower will want to make Royal Naples their home away from home.

By contrast, Chiaia is a bit like the prettiest girl at school – she accepts only the best hotels, exclusive boutiques and the most fashionable of residents. Squished between the waterfront and the hills of Vomero, it stretches along the Bay of Naples until it meets the more suburban trappings of Mergellina. Combine visits to the big names such as Gucci and Valentino with stops inside some of the more local purveyors of luxury goods to get the Italian look.

SIGHTS & ATTRACTIONS

Castel dell'Ovo

This imposing castle is Naples' oldest, boasting a history of over 1,000 years. Built during the Norman reign, the Castel dell'Ovo was originally intended for military use, but wound up housing a monastic community during the Middle Ages. Many of the rooms are now offices used by the military. However, there are still plenty of sections open to the public. Be sure to climb the ramp inside the castle to reach a platform with views of the Bay below.

ⓐ Via Partenope ❶ 081 240 0055 ● 09.00–sunset Mon–Sat, 09.00–13.30 Sun ⓝ Bus: 140, C24, C25, C28, R3; Tram: 1

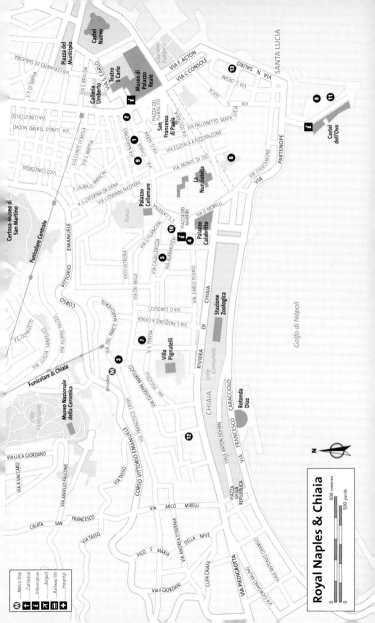

Royal Naples & Chiaia

Castel Nuovo
Piazza del Municipio
VIA CERVANTES DE SAAVEDRA
P. DI TAPPIA
VIA LUNGO TEATRO NUOVO
VICO CONCORDIA
VIA LUNGO NUOVO CELSO
Galleria Umberto
VIA S. CARLO
Teatro S. Carlo
VIA S. BRIGIDA
Museo di Palazzo Reale
i
2
VIA A. D'ISIA
VIA CONTE DI MOLA
VIA S. MATTIA
VIA NARDONES
VIA TOLEDO
VIA SERRA
1
PIAZZA DEL PLEBISCITO
San Francesco di Paola
VIA EGIZIACA A PIZZOFALCONE
VIA PALLONETTO SANTA
9
V. LAURA O. MANCINI
V. S. CATERINA DA SIENA
VIA GIOVANNI NICOTERA
Palazzo Cellamare
VIA S. CATERINA
VIA MONTE DI DIO
La Nunziatella
6
VIA F. ACTON
VIA C. CONSOLE
LUCIA
VIA N. SAURO
VIA C. ORSINI
SANTA LUCIA
13
9 **11**
i
Castel dell'Ovo
VIA CHIATAMONE
PARTENOPE
VIA
VIA
Certosa-Museo di San Martino
Funicolare Centrale
CORSO VITTORIO EMANUELE
VIA G. FILANGIERI
VICO VETRERIA
VIA CAVALLERIZZA
VIA ALABARDIERI
PIAZZA DEI MARTIRI
Palazzo Calabritto
VIA D. MORELLI
10
4
i
VIA DE MILLE
VIA CARLO POERIO
V.G. DONIZETTI
VIA DEL PARCO MARGHERITA
VIA FILIPPO PALIZZI
VIA G. CAROUCCI
VIA S. PASQUALE A CHIAIA
VIA S TERESA
Villa Pignatelli
7
Stazione Zoologica
CHIAIA
RIVIERA
DI
Villa Comunale
VIA
VIA LUCIA SANFELICE
Funicolare di Chiaia
Amedeo
M
3
VIA GIUSEPPE MARTUCCI
VIA M. TENNELLA
VIA ANTON DOHRN
CARACCIOLO
Rotonda Diaz
Golfo di Napoli
Museo Nazionale della Ceramica
Villa Floridiana
VIA LUCA GIORDANO
VIA A VACCARO
VIA ANIELLO FALCONE
VIA TASSO
CORSO VITTORIO EMANUELE
VIA FRANCESCO CRISPI
VIA PICCOLA
12
VIALE ANTON DOHRN
VIA FRANCESCO
PIAZZA DELLA REPUBBLICA
CALATA SAN FRANCESCO
VIA TASSO
VIA ARCO MIRELLI
VICO S. MARIA
VIA ANDREA D'ISERNIA
VIA DELLA NEVE
CUPA CAIAFA
VIA F GIORDANI
VIALE ANTONIO GRAMSCI
VIA PIEDIGROTTA

Key
Metro Stop
Cathedral
Information
Airport
Railway Stn
Hospital

N

0   500 metres
0   500 yards

Castel Nuovo

Castel Nuovo, built in 1279 by Charles of Anjou, was given its name to distinguish it from the older Castel dell'Ovo. Alterations performed in the 15th century have erased most of the original decoration. However, original Angevin architecture can still be seen in the form of the Cappella Palatina.

ⓐ Piazza Municipio ⓣ 081 420 1241 ⓛ 09.00–19.00 Mon–Sat June–Mar; 09.00–19.00 Mon–Sat, 09.00–14.00 Sun, Apr–May; ticket office closes 1 hr earlier ⓜ Bus: C25, E3, R1, R2, R3; Tram: 1

Giardini Pubblici

While the gardens are looking a bit ragged, this park is still a special place to enjoy a romantic stroll. Spectacular views of the bay.

ⓐ Via F. Acton ⓣ No phone ⓛ 07.00–24.00 May–Oct; 07.00–22.00 Nov–Apr ⓜ Bus: 24, C22, C82, R2, R3

△ *The Castel dell'Ovo stands guard over the city*

La Nunziatella

Built for the Bourbons in 1787, this tiny church features a beautiful marble altar and unique tile flooring. Today, the church is owned and used by the military academy located next door.

ⓐ Via Generale Parisi 16 ⓣ 081 764 1451 ⓛ 09.00–10.00 Sun for mass; all other times by appointment only Bus: 140, C24, C25, C28, R3; Tram: 1

Palazzo Reale

Construction on the Royal Palace began in 1600 and took two years to complete. Then, throughout the reign of the Spanish viceroys, additions were made. The Bourbons extended the *palazzo* in the mid-18th century, while the French gave the interiors its current neoclassical appearance.

For a building this size, it's surprising that the art collection is so poor. Instead, it's the architecture that inspires. Worth hunting for are the ornate private Teatrino di Corte theatre and the reading rooms of the Biblioteca Nazionale.

ⓐ Piazza del Plebiscito ⓣ 848 800 288, followed by 0 ⓛ 09.00–20.00 Mon, Tues, Thur–Sun; ticket office closes 1 hr earlier Bus: 24, C22, C82, R2, R3

Piazza del Plebiscito

Naples' largest public, pedestrianised square hosts New Year celebrations, music concerts, open-air theatre, buskers and political rallies. The surrounding Doric columns and equestrian statues dedicated to the kings of the Bourbon dynasty are popular meeting points.

ⓐ Piazza del Plebiscito Bus: 24, C22, C82, R2, R3

San Francesco di Paola

Naples has a lot of churches, but very few of them were built in the neoclassical style. San Francesco di Paola is the major exception – and is not much liked by locals for this reason. The church is a simple, yet majestic imitation of Rome's Pantheon, often marred by political graffiti.

ⓐ Piazza del Plebiscito ⓣ 081 764 5133 ⓛ 08.00–noon, 15.30–17.00 Mon–Sat, 08.00–13.00 Sun ⓝ Bus: 24, C22, C82, R2, R3

Stazione Zoologica

The Stazione Zoologica is one of Europe's oldest aquariums founded in 1872. The original 24 tanks still stand, housing many regional species including octopuses, seahorses and various fish. Legend has it that the liberating forces of 1944 held a victory banquet in the aquarium featuring a menu of its entire edible population.

ⓐ Villa Comunale, Riviera di Chiaia ⓣ 081 583 3111 ⓛ 09.00–18.00 Tues–Sat, 09.30–19.30 Sun, Mar–Oct; 09.00–17.00 Tues–Sat, 09.00–14.00 Sun, Nov–Feb ⓝ Bus: 140, 152, C28, R3; Tram: 1

Villa Comunale

This park, designed by Luigi Vanvitelli in 1781, was originally reserved strictly for royalty. Today, it is the city's most well-loved stretch of greenery. A bandstand, built in 1867, occasionally hosts public concerts and performances.

ⓐ Riviera di Chiaia ⓣ No phone ⓛ 07.00–24.00 May–Oct; 07.00–22.00 Nov–Apr ⓝ Bus: 140, 152, C28, R3; Tram: 1

Villa Pignatelli

Ferdinand Acton, son of the British prime minister Sir John Acton, built this villa in the 19th century, complete with an English-style garden. The Italian government took over in 1952 and now showcases a collection of porcelain figurines and busts. Landscape paintings are also in abundance, particularly in Room 6.

ⓐ Riviera di Chiaia 200 ⓣ 081 669 675 ⓛ 09.00–14.00 Tues–Sun Ⓝ Bus: 140, 152, C28, R3

RETAIL THERAPY

Shopping streets & markets

The main shopping streets can all be found in Chiaia, as most of the boutiques in Royal Naples are heavily geared towards tourist tat. The exception to this is Galleria Umberto. This covered shopping centre may remind some visitors of the Galleria in Milan. That said, it is much less up-market but it's a good place for a wander on a rainy day.

Chiaia's via Calabritto holds the bulk of designer names, including Armani, Gucci, Versace, Max Mara and Vuitton. For a more local experience, head to Chiaia's two markets: the Bancarelle a San Pasquale and the Fiera Antiquaria Napoletana. Located between via San Pasquale and via Carducci, the Bancarelle sells a wide selection of food, spices, fish, clothing and inexpensive jewellery on Mondays, Wednesdays, Fridays and Saturdays. The Fiera Antiquaria Napoletana is held much less frequently on the last Sunday of the month, excluding August. Sellers set up along the Riviera di Chiaia, offering furniture, paintings, porcelain and jewellery.

De Nobili Exclusive pieces in gold, coral and precious stone. Pieces can be commissioned according to individual specifications. ⓐ Via Filangieri 16B ⓣ 081 421 685 ⓦ www.denobili.com ⓛ 10.00–13.30, 16.30–20.00 Mon–Sat; closed Aug Ⓝ Bus: C25; Tram: 1, 4

Eddy Monetti Truly classic Italian clothing. Considered the ultimate in quality and timelessness. A true institution.
Menswear: @ Via dei Mille 45 ☏ 081 407 064. ⓦ www.eddymonetti.it
Ⓝ Funicular: Chiaia to Parco Margherita; Metro: Piazza Amedeo; Bus: C25
Womenswear: @ Piazzetta Santa Caterina 8 ☏ 081 403 229
🕐 09.30–13.30, 16.30–20.00 Mon–Sat; closed Mon am in winter, 2 wks Aug Ⓝ Bus: C25; Tram: 1, 4

Frette Luxury linens, towels and more. Very expensive but very worth it. @ Via dei Mille 2 ☏ 081 418 728 🕐 10.00–13.00, 16.30–20.00 Mon–Sat Ⓝ Funicular: Chiaia to Parco Margherita; Metro: Piazza Amedeo; Bus: C25

La Bottega della Ceramica Beautiful handmade ceramics collected from across Southern Italy. Prices are very reasonable. @ Via Carlo Poerio 40 ☏ 081 764 2626 🕐 09.30–13.30, 4.30–20.00 Mon–Sat; closed Aug Ⓝ Bus: C25; Tram: 1, 4

Lo Stock Discontinued and end-of-season designer labels for less. Be prepared to rummage. @ Via Fiorelli 7 ☏ 081 240 5253
🕐 10.00–13.30, 16.30–20.00 Mon–Sat; closed 2 wks Aug Ⓝ Funicular: Chiaia to Parco Margherita; Metro: Piazza Amedeo; Bus: C25

Marinella Top ties and accessories for the man who has everything. @ Riviera di Chiaia 287A ☏ 081 245 1182 ⓦ www.marinellanapoli.it
🕐 06.30–13.30, 16.00–20.00 Mon–Sat; closed 2 wks Aug Ⓝ Bus: C28; Tram: 1, 4

◀ *The Galleria Umberto is a beautiful place to shop*

Maxi Ho Fashion-forward designer duds from the likes of Prada and Dolce & Gabbana. @ Via Nisco 20 📞 081 414 721 🕐 09.30–13.00, 16.30–20.00 Mon–Sat; closed 1 wk Aug 🚇 Funicular: Chiaia to Parco Margherita; Metro: Piazza Amedeo; Bus: C25

Penna & Carta 1989 When was the last time you wrote a letter? Be inspired by the handmade stationery and hand-blown glass pens at this boutique. @ Largo Vasto a Chiaia 86 📞 081 418 724 🕐 10.00–13.30, 16.30–20.00 Mon–Sat; closed Aug 🚇 Bus: C25; Tram: 1, 4

Siola High-end, designer maternity and children's wear purveyor. Labels include Armani and Pinko Pallino. @ Via Chiaia 111–15 📞 081 412 580 🕐 10.00–13.30, 16.30–20.00 Mon–Sat; closed Sat pm (summer), Mon am (winter), and 2 wks in Aug 🚇 Bus: C25; Tram: 1, 4

TAKING A BREAK

Brandi ❶ Probably Naples' most famous *pizzeria*, Brandi claims to have invented the pizza Margherita in honour of Italy's Queen Margherita in 1889. Famous diners have included ex-US president Bill Clinton. @ Salita Sant'Anna di Palazzo 1 📞 081 416 928 🌐 www.brandi.it 🕐 12.30–15.00, 19.30–24.00; closed 1 wk Aug 🚇 Bus: C22, C25, R2

Caffè Gambrinus ❷ The service is haughty, the menu expensive, and the revolutionaries and poets are long gone. So why does Gambrinus remain the most popular café in Naples? Location, location, location. That, combined with the art deco interiors and a

A SLICE IS NICE

Neapolitan chefs claim that the world's favourite fast food was invented in the wood-fired ovens of this city. Making pizza in Naples is a task that has been elevated to an art form. Residents of various neighbourhoods have been known to battle over which *pizzeria* makes the best slices in town.

Once a meal reserved for the poor, the Neapolitan pizza is now enjoyed by everyone. But you won't find the doughy crusts favoured outside of Italy; it's thin, crisp, dry crusts that are the speciality in this town.

The best *pizzerias* will always have long queues snaking from their doors at all times of the day.

Traditional local choices include:

Caprese: Fresh cherry tomatoes and mozzarella. A few leaves of *rucola* or *rughetta* (rocket) are optional.

Capricciosa: Tomato, black olives, artichokes and ham.

Margherita: Tomato, mozzarella, basil and oil.

Marinara: Tomato, oregano, garlic and oil.

Prosciutto crudo e rucola in bianco: Parma ham, mozzarella and fresh rocket.

Ripieno: A pizza folded pastry-style stuffed with mozzarella, ricotta and salami topped with tomato and basil.

Ripieno fritto: A deep-fried version of the *Ripieno*.

Salsiccia e friarielli: Mozzarella, sausage and *friarielli* (a local variety of spinach).

past that included customers such as Oscar Wilde. ➌ Via Chiaia 1–2 ❶ 081 417 582 ● 08.00–01.30. ⓝ Funicular: Centrale to Augusteo; Bus: 24, C22, C25, C57

Caffè Amadeus ❸ The large number of outside tables on the Piazza Amedeo is the main draw of this café. Perfect for watching the romancing couples of Naples ride by on their Vespas. Ⓐ Piazza Amedeo 5 ❶ 081 761 3023 ❷ 07.00–03.00 Ⓝ Metro: Amedeo; Bus: C24, C25

La Caffettiera ❹ This elegant café is popular with the blue-rinse set due to the inspiring interiors and old-fashioned service. Staff consider it a rival to the Caffè Gambrinus, yet it attracts only a fraction of the tourists of its more centrally located competition. Ⓐ Piazza dei Martiri 30 ❶ 081 764 4243 ❷ 08.00–21.30 Mon–Fri, 08.00–22.00 Sat & Sun; closed 2 wks Aug Ⓝ Bus: C25

La Focaccia Express ❺ Choose from an incredible selection of pizza slices and focaccia if a quick bite is all you're after. For the freshest choices, watch what comes out of the oven before you place your order. Ⓐ Vico Belledonne a Chiaia 31 ❶ 081 412 277 ❷ 10.00–02.00 Mon–Sat, 18.00–03.00 Sun; closed 3 wks Aug Ⓝ Bus: C22, C25

Vinarium ❻ For a leisurely glass of wine, Vinarium is the place to go. There is a nice selection of medium-priced bottles to choose from. Food is rather lacklustre. Be prepared to queue on weekends. Ⓐ Vico Santa Maria Cappella Vecchia 7 ❶ 081 764 4114 ❷ 11.00–16.30, 19.00–01.30 Mon–Sat Sept–June; 12.00–16.00 Mon–Sat July; closed Aug

❶ *The Neptune fountain in the via Medina*

AFTER DARK

Restaurants

Osteria da Tonino £–££ ❼ This casual *osterie* offers tasty dishes on a budget. A great place to go for a casual, yet flavoursome meal.
🄰 Via Santa Teresa a Chiaia 47 🄲 081 421 533 🄻 12.30–16.00 Mon–Wed, Sun, 12.30–16.00, 08.00–13.00 Thur–Sat Oct–May; 12.30–16.00 Mon–Sat June, July, Sept; closed Aug 🄝 Funicular: Chiaia to Parco Marcherita; Metro: Amedeo; Bus: C24, C25, C26, C27, C28

Ciro ££ ❽ While the food isn't fabulous – stick with the fish dishes to be safe – it's the views that make this restaurant so worthwhile. Located almost at the base of the Castel dell'Ovo, it's a delightful eatery from which to enjoy the sun set over the waters of the bay.
🄰 Borgo Marinaro 29–30 🄲 081 764 6006 🄦 www.ristoranteciro.it 🄻 12.30–15.30, 19.30–24.00 Mon, Tues, Thur–Sun 🄝 Bus: C25

La Stanza del Gusto ££ ❾ Located just off the busy via Chiaia at the top of a flight of stairs, this lovely find serves a menu of seasonal dishes that changes every day – so if you like it the first time, you can come back again and again. Warm, friendly and delicious.
🄰 Vicoletto Sant'Arpino 21 🄲 081 401 578 🄻 20.00–23.00 Mon–Sat; closed 3 wks July–Aug 🄝 Bus: 140, C9, C18, C22, C25

Umberto ££ ❿ The only vegetarian restaurant in town worth mentioning. The food is flavoursome and challenging dietary requirements can be catered for. Gluten-free food is also available.
🄰 Via Alabardieri 30/31 🄲 081 418 555 🄦 www.umberto.it 🄻 12.00–16.00, 19.00–23.00 Tues–Sun; closed 3 wks Aug

Zi Teresa ££ ⓫ This family-run eatery has been dishing out delicious seafood since 1916. Locals love it for special gatherings such as christenings and anniversaries. As such, it's often full with large groups. Tables overlooking the port are the most coveted. Advance booking is recommended, especially for Sunday lunch. ⓐ Borgo Marinaro 1 ⓣ 081 764 2565 ⓦ www.ziteresa.it ⓛ 12.30–15.30, 20.00–23.30 Tues–Sat, 12.30–16.00 Sun; closed lunch 1 wk Aug ⓝ Bus: C25

Dora £££ ⓬ If you're going to splurge, then do it here. This tiny restaurant offers the best fish in town. Bookings are a necessity. ⓐ Via Ferdinando Palasciano 30 ⓣ 081 680 519 ⓛ 12.30–15.00, 20.00–24.00 Mon–Sat; closed 3 wks Aug ⓝ Bus: 140, C9, C18, C24, C25, C28

La Cantinella £££ ⓭ For a blow-out meal, this is the restaurant Neapolitans choose for special occasions. The quality of the seafood is uniformly excellent; however, the sauces and accompaniments can sometimes prove to be overpowering. Service is first class, yet formal. A jacket and tie will be required. ⓐ Via Nazario Sauzo 23 ⓣ 081 764 8684 ⓦ www.lacantinella.it ⓛ 12.30–15.00, 19.30–23.30 Mon–Sat; closed 2 wks Aug ⓝ Bus: C25

Bars, clubs & discos
Enoteca Belledonne This minuscule bar gets packed every night with the upper middle classes who call Chiaia home. If you find crowds difficult, don't even think about going anytime between 19.00 and 21.00, when seats are at a premium. ⓐ Vico Belledonne a Chiaia 18 ⓣ 081 403 162 ⓛ 18.00–24.00; closed Aug ⓝ Metro: Amedeo; Bus: C25, R3

Marshall Lounge For lovers of minimalist chic, a la Starck, this tiny bar should be on your must drink list. The flawless surroundings attract those more into looking cool than feeling comfortable. ⓐ Vicoletto Belledonne a Chiaia 12 ⓣ 081 405 216 ⓛ 18.00–02.00 Tues–Sun; closed July–Sept ⓜ Metro: Amedeo; Bus: C25, R3

Otto Jazz A local haunt that attracts fans of traditional jazz. Performers tend to come from the surrounding region and are of good standard. ⓐ Salita Cariati 23 ⓣ 081 551 3765 ⓛ 23.00–02.00 Fri–Sun; closed July, Aug ⓜ Funicular: Centrale to corso Vittorio Emanuele; Bus: C16

S'move Definitely the hottest place in town for a drink. There's no dance floor but the beats do get booties moving. While the space may be filled by 'the beautiful people', the atmosphere is welcoming. ⓐ Vico dei Sospiri 10A ⓣ 081 764 5813 ⓦ www.smove-lab.net ⓛ 14.00–04.00 Mon, 19.00–04.00 Tues–Sat, 19.00–04.00 Sun Sept–mid-June; 20.00–04.00 last 2 wks June, July; closed Aug ⓜ Metro: Amedeo; Bus: C25, R3

Cinemas & theatres
Amedeo Small, thin space that shows films in English on Thursdays. ⓐ Via Martucci 69 ⓣ 081 680 266 ⓜ Metro: Amedeo; Bus: C24, C25

Mercadente Naples' main theatrical performance space has been in existence since 1779. Some of Italy's best-known actors can often be found here treading the boards. ⓐ Piazza Municipio 1 ⓣ 081 551 3396 ⓦ www.teatrostabilenapoli.it ⓛ Box office open

10.30–13.00, 17.30–19.30 Tues–Sun late Sept–Apr. Performances 21.00
Wed, Fri, Sat, 17.30, 21.00 Thur, 18.00 Sun late Sept–Apr ❷ Bus: 24, C22,
C25, C57

Politeama Characterless performance space that often hosts
modern dance and live music. Also known to stage contemporary
opera for Teatro San Carlo. ❸ Via Monte di Dio 80 ❶ 081 764 5001
❶ Box office open 10.30–13.30, 16.30–19.30 Mon–Sat Oct–May
on performance days. Performances 21.00 Tues, Wed, Sat & Sun
❷ Bus: C22

Teatro San Carlo The second-best opera house in Italy. Only Milan's
La Scala can compete – and many say it's a close call. In operation
since 1736, this stunning theatre is actually a replacement built in
1816 following a devastating fire. Performances tend to be
traditional and of high quality. Premieres bring out the who's who
of Neapolitan society. ❸ Via San Carlo 98F ❶ 081 797 2331
❶ www.teatrosancarlo.it ❶ Box office open 10.00–15.00 Tues–Sun
Sept–May; 10.00–15.00 Tues–Fri June, July and 1 hr before
performances ❷ Bus: 24, C22, C25, C57

Villa Pignatelli This luxurious villa showcases double bills that
combine old and new, and well known with rarity. Most films are
screened in their original language. ❸ Riviera di Chiaia 200
❶ 081 425 037 ❶ www.galleriatoledo.com ❷ Bus: C28, R3

Warner Village Metropolitan Napoli Big Hollywood blockbusters
in a typical multiplex setting. ❸ Via Chiaia 149 ❶ 081 252 5133
❶ www.warnervillage.it ❷ Bus: C25, R2

Centro Storico & La Sanità

For many years, the city of Naples was just the Centro Storico. Bound by the city walls, thousands of residents packed into its tight, winding streets to live in what was at one time the most populated city on the planet. These winding streets remain, giving the area its strong neighbourhood character – especially in Spaccanapoli, the collection of pedestrianised, laundry-clad streets that slice the area in two.

● *The busy streets of Spaccanapoli*

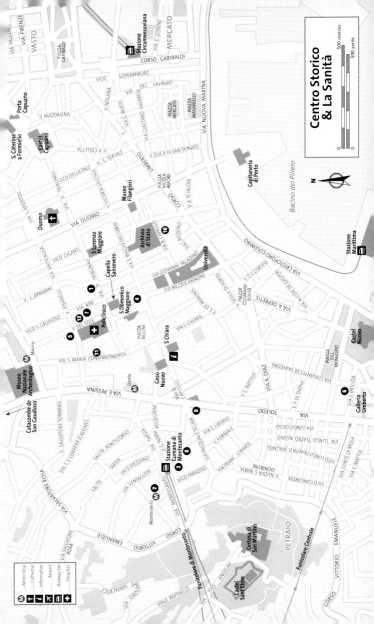

MAXIMISING ON TIME

❶ If you have just one day to spend in Naples, then this is the district to explore. Packed with churches, archaeological sites and one of Naples' most renowned museums, it's a living history and anthropology lesson – but a lot more fun than any lecture!

SIGHTS & ATTRACTIONS

Cappella Sansevero

The funerary chapel of the Di Sangro family is known best for the macabre figures in the crypt. Legend has it that they are the dead bodies of the family's domestic staff.

ⓐ Via Francesco de Sanctis 19 ❶ 081 551 8470 ❶ 10.00–16.40 Mon, Wed–Sat, 10.00–13.00 Sun, Nov–Apr; 10.00–17.40 Mon, Wed–Sat, 10.00–13.00 Sun, May–Oct Ⓝ Metro: Dante or Montesanto; Bus: E1

Catacombe di San Gaudioso

This extensive subterranean collection of catacombs holds the remains of St Gaudiosus, a 5th-century North African bishop. His burial here has transformed the labyrinthine cave system into an important shrine and place of holy pilgrimage. Fans of the macabre will appreciate the displays chronicling ancient burial practices. Tours depart from the church of the Santa Maria della Sanità across the street.

ⓐ Via Sanità 124 ❶ 081 544 1305
Ⓦ www.santamariadellasanita.it ❶ Church: 08.30–12.30, 17.00–20.00 Mon–Sat, 08.30–13.30 Sun; Catacombs: guided tours 09.30, 10.15, 11.00, 11.45, 12.30 Ⓝ Metro: Cavour or Museo; Bus: C51, C52

Duomo

Housing the remains of Naples' patron saint San Gennaro, the *duomo* is the most important cathedral in the city. Its history can be dated back to the 4th century, but the structure that stands today was built in the 13th century over the remains of two previous houses of worship. San Gennaro's feast day on 19 September is the biggest day in the cathedral's calendar when vials of his blood liquefy in an annual miracle.

ⓐ Via Duomo 147 ① 081 449 097 ⓦ www.duomodinapoli.com
🕒 Church: 08.00–12.30, 16.30–19.00 Mon–Sat, 08.00–13.30, 17.00–19.30 Sun; archaeological area & baptistery: 09.00–12.00, 16.30–18.30 Mon–Sat, 08.30–13.00 Sun Ⓜ Bus: E1, R2

Gesù Nuovo

Originally a *palazzo*, this church is notable for its façade of raised, diamond-shaped stone. The interiors were transformed from a place of worship in the 16th century. Of particular interest is the room dedicated to local saint Giuseppe Moscati, a 20th-century Neapolitan doctor who forsook the trappings of wealth and prestige in order to tend to the health of the local poor.

ⓐ Piazza del Gesù Nuovo 2 ① 081 551 8613 🕒 07.00–12.30, 16.00–19.00 Mon–Sat, 07.00–13.30, 16.00–19.00 Sun Ⓜ Metro: Montesanto or Dante; Bus: E1, R1

San Lorenzo Maggiore

Take a trip back in time to Graeco–Roman Neapolis and wander the ancient streets of Naples discovered under the church in what is truly the most wondrous ancient site in the city. Excavation work is ongoing, but a butcher's shop, bakery, dyer's stall and porticoed arcade are all accessible.

⊕ Via Dei Tribunali 316 ☎ 081 211 0860
ⓦ www.sanlorenzomaggiore.it 🕐 09.00–17.00 Mon–Sat,
09.30–13.30 Sun Ⓜ Metro: Dante or Montesanto; Bus: E1

Santa Chiara

This Gothic church was built during the reign of Robert of Anjou.
World War II bombs and baroque-era reconstruction have done
much to reduce this place of worship favoured by the aristocracy –
after the war, all that was left were the four walls. Since restored,
the damage can still be spotted if you go past the cloister. There, you
will find salvaged pieces from the original 14th-century structure
and various shards of shrapnel.

⊕ Via Benedetto Croce ☎ 081 552 6280 ⓦ www.oltreilchiostro.org
🕐 Church: 08.00–12.30, 16.30–19.30; museum & cloister:
09.30–13.00, 14.30–17.30 Mon–Sat, 09.30–13.00 Sun Ⓜ Metro: Dante
or Montesanto; Bus: E1

CULTURE

Museo Nazionale Archeologico

This former *palazzo* that once housed Naples University was
converted by King Ferdinand I into a private art gallery after he
inherited hundreds of ancient pieces from his grandmother. Following
the discovery of the ruins at Pompeii, the rooms quickly filled up.
Today's museum showcases just a fraction of its possessions.

Boasting one of the most important collections of Roman
antiquities in the world, the Museo Nazionale is truly the crown
jewel of all the museums in the city. The bulk of the treasures
taken from Herculaneum and Pompeii can be found on the first
floor centred on the Sala Meridiana. Attempts to bring in younger

visitors have resulted in a number of temporary exhibits in the rooms off the main courtyard. Recent artists profiled include Jeff Koons and Damien Hirst.

ⓐ Piazza Museo 19 ⓣ 081 564 8941
ⓦ www.archeona.arti.beniculturali.it ⓛ Museum: 09.00–19.30 Mon, Wed–Sun; ticket office closes 1 hr earlier ⓜ Metro: Cavour or Museo; Bus: 47, CS, E1

🔺 *The* duomo *is Naples' most important church*

RETAIL THERAPY

Shopping streets & markets

For many, the highlight of a visit to the Centro Storico and La Sanità is the shopping. The street scenes and service draw them, as each boutique has quirky characteristics that make shopping fun.

The high street shops of the via Toledo are in converted *palazzi* once owned by the wealthy of the city. The exteriors alone are worth a spot of browsing.

Centro Storico is all about life and passion. Shopping here is a lesson in Italian communication – especially in the massive markets surrounding the via Pignasecca.

Antiche Delizie Foodies will love the mouth-watering selection of mozzarellas, antipasti, truffles and cured meats. Service is very friendly. ⓐ Via Pasquale Scura 14 ⓣ 081 551 3088 ⓛ 08.00–20.00 Mon–Wed, Fri, Sat, 08.00–15.00 Thur, 09.00–14.00 Sun; closed 1 wk Aug ⓝ Metro: Montesanto; Bus: 24, 105, R1

Arte in Oro Unique copies of classical Roman jewellery are made by two gifted brothers in this dusty boutique. The place to go for something special. ⓐ Via Benedetto Croce 20 ⓣ 081 551 6980 ⓛ 10.00–13.30, 16.30–19.30 Mon–Sat; closed 3 wks Aug ⓝ Metro: Dante; Bus: E1, R1, R2, R3, R4

> **TO START YOUR DAY …**
> Pick up a glass of freshly squeezed fruit juice or drink a coffee with the pyjama-clad patients of the nearby hospital before you wander the streets filled with cakes and clobber.

Enoteca Dante Family-owned wine shop that offers both local and imported varieties. Local vintages are a speciality, in addition to liquors and champagnes from across Italy and France. ⓐ Piazza Dante 18 ❶ 081 549 9689 ⓛ 09.00–20.30 Mon–Sat; closed 2 wks Aug ⓜ Metro: Dante or Montesanto; Bus: 24, 105, R1

Garlic Not for the fashion faint-hearted, Garlic showcases the new, the adventurous and the just plain wild. Everything from shoes to clothes is on sale from a wide array of young design talent. ⓐ Via Toledo 111 ❶ 081 5524 4966 ⓛ 09.30–13.00, 16.30–20.00 Mon–Sat; closed 2 wks Aug ⓜ Metro: Montesanto; Bus: 24, 105, R1

La Rinascente This branch of the Italian department store chain is located in a converted *palazzo* on the via Toledo. Good for basics and household goods. ⓐ Via Toledo 340 ❶ 081 411 511 ⓛ 09.00–20.00 Mon–Sat, 10.00–14.00, 19.00–20.00 Sun ⓜ Funicular: Centrale to Augusteo; Metro: Diaz; Bus: R1, R2, R4

Marco Ferrigno Many people come to Naples purely with the intention of purchasing Nativity figurines. When you see the terracotta offerings at this cave-like boutique, you will understand why. Highly collectable. ⓐ Via San Gregorio Armeno 10 ❶ No phone ⓛ 09.30–13.30, 16.00–20.00 Mon–Sat; closed 3 wks Aug ⓜ Bus: E1

Napoli Mania For souvenirs that are a step up from the usual tat, head to this witty boutique in the heart of the via Toledo. Everything from t-shirts to coffee mugs is on sale – many featuring jokes and expressions in Neapolitan dialect. ⓐ Via Toledo 312–313 ❶ 081 414 120 ⓛ 10.00–13.45, 16.30–20.00 Mon–Sat Jan–Apr,

June–Nov; 10.00–13.45, 16.30–20.00 May, Dec; closed Sun in Aug
Ⓝ Funicular: Centrale to Augusteo; Bus: C25, R2

Talarico Naples' oldest handicraft shop. The owners pride
themselves on keeping the tricks of local craftsmanship and
artisan work alive. Ⓐ Vico Due Porte a Toledo 4/B Ⓣ 081 401 979
Ⓦ www.mariotalarico.com Ⓛ 09.30–13.30, 16.00–20.00 Mon–Sat;
closed Aug Ⓝ Bus: C28; Tram: 1, 4

TAKING A BREAK

Di Matteo ❶   Don't be put off eating at this *pizzeria*. While the
décor is nothing to write home about, the slices are. Ⓐ Via dei
Tribunali 94 Ⓣ 081 455 262 Ⓛ 10.00–24.00 Mon–Sat; open in Dec;
closed 2 wks Aug Ⓝ Metro: Dante; Bus: R1, R2

Friggitoria Firoenzano ❷   Tasty snacks that make a change from
the usual slices of pizza. When in season, the deep-fried artichokes
are heavenly. Ⓐ Piazza Montesanto 6 Ⓣ No phone Ⓛ 08.00–22.00
Mon–Sat; closed 2 wks Aug Ⓝ Metro: Montesanto

Gelateria della Scimmia ❸   Naples' oldest and most established
gelaterie. While there are dozens of delicious ice cream flavours to
choose from, the basics such as strawberry and lemon are usually the
best. Ⓐ Piazza Carità 4 Ⓣ 081 552 0272 Ⓛ 10.00–22.30 Mon, Tues, Thur,
Fri, 10.00–01.00 Sat & Sun, Jan–Mar, Nov; 10.00–24.00 Apr–Oct, Dec
Ⓝ Funicular: Centrale to Augusteo; Metro: Montesanto; Bus: R1, E3

Gran Caffè Aragonese ❹   This popular café is a favourite of local
artists, buskers and students. A lively crowd, drawn by the tasty

sweets and savouries, is always guaranteed. A great place for a well-deserved rest. ② Piazza San Domenico Maggiore 5/8 ❶ 081 552 8740 ⓦ www.grancaffearagonese.it 🕓 08.00–24.00 Ⓜ Metro: Museo or Piazza Cavour; Bus: CS, E1, R2

AFTER DARK

Restaurants

Cantina della Sapienza £ ❺ If you don't get an invitation to a Neapolitan home for a meal, then a stop at the Cantina della Sapienza is the next best thing. The daily changing menu hosts both intriguing original dishes and local favourites. Service is friendly. The desserts and local red wine are especially recommended. ② Via della Sapienza 40 ❶ 081 459 078 🕓 12.00–15.30 Mon–Sat; closed 3 wks Aug Ⓜ Metro: Piazza Cavour; Bus: C57, R4

Ciro a Santa Brigida £ ❻ While this eatery is technically a restaurant, it's best known for its pizza. Sit down and enjoy choosing from a menu that offers out-of-the-ordinary possibilities such as seafood pizza. Service is traditional, but the wine list is strong. ② Via Santa Brigida 71 ❶ 081 552 4072 🕓 12.30–15.30, 19.30–24.00 Mon– Sat; closed 2 wks Aug Ⓜ Funicular: Centrale to Augusteo; Bus: C25, R2

La Locanda del Grifo £ ❼ Traditional fare served in a convenient Centro Storico location. All the dishes are excellent and set off nicely by the selection of local wines. Try and snag an outdoor table if the weather is good. ② Via F del Giudice 14 ❶ 081 442 0815 🕓 12.00–15.30, 19.00–23.30 Mon, Wed–Sun Jan–Oct; 12.00–15.30, 19.00–23.30 Nov, Dec Ⓜ Metro: Dante; Bus: R1, R4

La Vecchia Cantina £ ❽ A delightful *osterie* serving local specialities. As it's located next to the fish market, seafood dishes are good choices. ⓐ Via San Nicola alla Carità 13–14 ❶ 081 552 0226 ⓐ 12.00–15.30, 20.00–23.00 Mon, Wed–Sat; 12.00–15.30 Tues, Sun; closed 2 wks Aug Ⓝ Metro: Dante or Montesanto; Bus: C57, R1, R4

Hosteria Toledo £–££ ❾ Simple, traditional dishes and local wine served in simple surroundings. ⓐ Vico Giardinetto a Toledo 78, off via Toledo ❶ 081 421 257 ❶ 12.00–15.00, 20.00–24.00 Mon, Wed–Sun; 12.00–15.00 Tues Ⓝ Funicular: Centrale to Via Rima; Bus: C25, R2

Antica Osteria Pisano ££ ❿ This tiny eatery is extremely popular and often packed. Traditional Neapolitan dishes are its speciality. If you're a foodie, take advantage of the fact that the kitchen opens up onto the restaurant and ask for a tour. ⓐ Piazzetta Crocelle ai Mannesi 1 ❶ 081 554 8325 ❶ 12.00–16.00, 19.00–23.00 Mon–Sat; closed 2 wks Aug Ⓝ Metro: Dante or Museo; Bus: R2

Bellini ££ ⓫ Enormous portions of seafood mixed with pasta. That's all they serve, and all you'll ever need. Absolutely fresh and delicious. ⓐ Via Santa Maria di Constantinopoli 79–80 ❶ 081 459 774 ❶ 12.30–15.30, 19.30–23.00 Mon–Sat July–Sept; 12.30–15.30, 19.30–23.00 Mon–Sat, 12.30–15.30 Sun, Oct–June; closed 1 wk Aug Ⓝ Metro: Dante

La Cantina del Sole ££ ⓬ For complete authenticity, this restaurant wins the battle. Most of the recipes can be dated back to the 17th and 18th centuries. Dishes are extremely hearty, filling and feature intriguing flavours. ⓐ Via Paladino 3 ❶ 081 552

7312 🕐 19.00–24.00 Mon, Wed–Sat, 13.00–15.30, 19.00–24.00 Sun; closed Aug Ⓜ Metro: Dante; Bus: R2

Bars, clubs & discos

Kinky Bar Contrary to its name, this bar is not made for the fetish set. Instead, it spins reggae beats for those who like dub music. In summer, the crowds spill out onto the adjoining alleyways. 🅰 Via Cisterna dell'Olio 21 🕿 081 552 1571 🕐 22.30–03.00; closed mid-June–Sept Ⓜ Metro: Dante; Bus: 24, R1, R2

A WALK THROUGH THE CENTRO STORICO

Begin your explorations at the *duomo*, home to Naples' patron saint. While this structure was built in the 13th century, a church of some sort has been sitting on this spot since the 4th century.

Turn left out of the *duomo* and take a right on the Via dei Tribunali to reach San Lorenzo Maggiore, another important church also known for its miracles – this time in the form of the perpetually liquid blood of San Lorenzo.

Continue along Via dei Tribunali until you get to San Gregorio Armeno. Three more saints have liquefying blood in this church – Santa Patrizia, San Giovanni Battista and San Panteleone. Are you beginning to notice a theme?

Leave San Gregorio Armeno by turning right at the end of the street onto Via San Biagio to shop the stalls selling nativity and *commedia dell'arte* figurines. At the end of the street, turn right onto the jeweller's street of Via Benedetto Croce. Both Santa Chiara and Gesù Nuovo will be on the right; otherwise turn right onto Via San Sebastiano to enjoy a coffee on the Piazza Bellini.

Rising South Naples' newest club opened in 2002 to great fanfare. Comfy armchairs and sofas mix well with the lounge music groove. Via San Sebastiano 19 📞 335 811 7107 🌐 www.risingsouth.com 🕐 22.00–03.00 Tues–Sun; closed June–mid-Oct Ⓝ Metro: Dante; Bus: 24, E1, R1, R2

Superfly A jazz soundtrack provides the tunes. The whiz of a bar provides the cocktails. You will, however, have to fight for one of the six stools in this postage stamp-sized bar. A good place to start the evening. Ⓐ Via Cisterna dell'Olio 12 📞 347 127 2178 🕐 19.00–03.00 Tues–Sun; closed June–Sept Ⓝ Metro: Dante; Bus: 24, R1, R2

Velvet Zone This dark and atmospheric nightclub is the best place to dance in the Centro Storico. DJs spin everything from funk to techno every day of the week. Smaller rooms that are just off from the main dance floor offer comfortable options if all you want to do is chat. Ⓐ Via Cisterna dell'Olio 11 📞 339 670 0234 🕐 23.00–04.00 Wed, Thur, Sun, 23.00–06.00 Fri, Sat; closed June–mid-Oct Ⓝ Metro: Dante; Bus: 24, E1, R1, R2

Cinemas & theatres

Bellini Beautifully redecorated theatre that stages everything from Broadway blockbuster musicals to local dance troupes. Mainstream entertainment constitutes the bulk of the programming. Ⓐ Via Conte di Ruvo 14–19 📞 081 549 9688 🌐 www.teatrobellini.it 🕐 Box office open 10.30–13.30, 17.00–20.00 Mon–Fri, 10.30–14.00 Sat, Oct–May. Performances 21.00 Tues–Sat, 17.30 Sun, Oct–May Ⓝ Metro: Cavour or Museo; Bus: 24, R1, R2

Elicantropo This 40-seat theatre hosts fringe theatre and young companies looking to try out modern theatre pieces. 🄐 Vico Gerolomini 3 🄣 081 296 640 🄦 www.teatroelicantropo.com 🄛 Box office open 17.30–20.00 Oct–May. Performances 21.00 Oct–May 🄜 Metro: Cavour or Museo; Bus: 149, CD, CS

Galeria Toledo A small modern theatre that programmes both cinema and new theatre projects. 🄐 Via Concezione a Montecalvario 34 🄣 081 425 824 🄦 www.galleriatoledo.com 🄛 Box office open 10.30–19.00 Tues–Sun Sept–May. Performances 20.30 Tues–Sun Oct–May 🄜 Metro: Montesanto; Bus: E2

Modernissimo This complex of four cinemas is a local favourite screening everything from Hollywood blockbusters to children's cartoons to arthouse classics. 🄐 Via Cisterna dell'Olio 59 🄣 081 551 1247 🄜 Metro: Dante; Bus: 24, R1, R2

Teatro Nuovo While this performance space has been here for only 20 years, it actually stands on the site of one of the city's oldest theatres. Programming is dedicated to the best new and international work. 🄐 Via Montecalvario 16 🄣 081 425 958 🄦 www.nuovoteatronuovo.it 🄛 Box office open from 17.00 on performance nights. Phone bookings 09.30–14.00, 17.00–19.00 Mon–Fri. Performances 21.00 Tues–Sat, 18.00 Sun, mid-Oct–May

Vomero & Capodimonte

Nothing much links the two neighbourhoods of Capodimonte and Vomero other than the fact they are both situated on the tops of hills. So why are we linking them together? To put it simply, it's because they are the most recent additions to Neapolitan neighbourhood life. Getting to Vomero and Capodimonte was always difficult due to their hilltop locations. Vomero became popular as an address only following the completion of the first funicular railway in 1889. This fact works to your benefit, as the views from both locales is superb.

What distinguishes both neighbourhoods from the city below is their relative peace and greenery. Capodimonte is sometimes seen as one massive park with the Museo situated in the centre. The grounds are a favourite spot for joggers, families and courting couples – especially at the weekend.

With its pedestrianised centre and cafés brimming with local residents, via Scarlatti is the place to go in Vomero. While the Centro Storico is all about vibrant Neapolitan life, Vomero is much more middle class and subdued – a great change of pace if you can't take the constantly loud street theatre of the older parts of the city.

SIGHTS & ATTRACTIONS

Castel Sant'Elmo

The Castel Sant'Elmo can probably boast Naples' most glorious views. While not the original structure, the current building owes much of its look to additions made in the 16th century when it gained its six-pointed star shape. A castle has existed at this strategic location overlooking the Bay of Naples since 1329 when

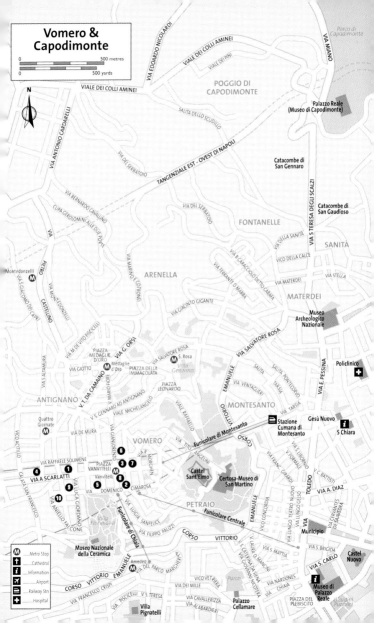

Robert of Anjou constructed a fortification above a small church dedicated to St Erasmus (or Elmo).

A walk through the castle can be strangely spooky, especially during the gloomy winter months. Periodic temporary modern and experimental art collections do much to brighten up the surroundings, including displays in the dungeons on the first

FUN ON THE FUNICULARS

Before the advent of the funicular railway in 1889, travellers to Vomero were forced to traverse a long flight of steps leading up from the city centre. Obviously, this limited many visitors from making the journey.

Rides on the funicular railway proved to be so popular that a famous song was composed in the late 19th century broadcasting its reputation. 'Funiculì, Funiculà' remains wildly popular and can still be heard on many recordings – especially in the streets of the city that sparked the craze.

In total, four lines run between Vomero and the districts below. The longest funicular is the Centrale line, which begins its journey on the via Toledo and terminates near the via Scarlatti.

As only two trains run on each line at any given time (one going up; the other down), it can get extremely busy – especially during the traditional rush hours. If the trains are packed, walking up the steps remains an option, but only for the physically fit. On temperate days, it remains an enjoyable (if slightly tiring) journey.

🄸 Tickets can be purchased from any of the funicular stations. Trains run every 10 minutes.

🔺 The Certosa-Museo di San Martino

floor. Breathtaking views can be enjoyed from the Piazza d'Armi on the roof.

📍 Via Tito Angelini 22 ☎ 081 578 4030 🕐 09.00–19.30 Tues–Sun; ticket office closes 1 hr earlier 🚡 Funicular: Montesanto to via Morghen, Centrale to Piazza Fuga or Chiaia to via Cimarosa; Bus: V1

Catacombe di San Gennaro

Lucky San Gennaro. Not only does he have a city in his thrall over two phials of his blood, he also gets to commune with the dead in a catacomb named after him. Two levels of catacombs contain some much-muddied frescoes dating back as far as the 2nd century AD. But it wasn't until the body of San Gennaro was brought here in the 5th century that the catacombs became a place of pilgrimage and worship.

ⓐ Via Capodimonte 16 ⓣ 081 741 1071 ⓛ guided tours only 09.00, 10.00, 11.00, 12.00 Tues–Sun ⓝ Bus: 24, 110, R2

CULTURE

Certosa-Museo di San Martino

The Museo di San Martino boasts one of the most intriguing collections of treasures in the city. To its credit, San Martino is more than just a museum. A former monastery, the grounds of the Certosa-Museo hold an art gallery, collection of Nativity scenes, and a church. The highlight of the collection is the fascinating *Tavola Strozzi*, a 3-D depiction of the city of Naples as it looked in the 15th century.

ⓐ Largo San Martino 5 ⓣ 081 558 5942 ⓛ 08.30–19.30 Tues–Sun; ticket office closes 1 hr earlier ⓝ Funicular: Montesanto to via Morghen, Centrale to Piazza Fuga or Chiaia to via Cimarosa; Bus: V1

Museo di Capodimonte

Second only to the Museo Nazionale, this wonderful art museum holds the paintings of the celebrated Farnese collection. A number of masterpieces, including works by Raphael and Titian, are showcased, including Titian's *Danae* located in Room 11. Other big names exhibited include Botticelli, El Greco, Renoir, Caravaggio, Rembrandt, Tintoretto and Breughels.

ⓐ Via Capodimonte ⓣ 081 749 9111 ⓛ 10.00–19.00 Tues–Sat, 09.00–14.00 Sun ⓝ Bus: 24, 110, R2

Museo Nazionale della Ceramica

The world of ceramics is celebrated in this museum. The first floor is dedicated to the history of European work, including examples from Meissen and fine Capodimonte figurines. The ground level holds international pieces with a focus on Japanese and Chinese items.

ⓐ Via Cimarosa 77 ❶ 081 578 1776 ⊙ guided tours only 09.30, 11.00, 12.30 Tues–Sun Ⓝ Funicular: Montesanto to via Morghen, Centrale to Piazza Fuga or Chiaia to via Cimarosa; Bus: E4, V1

RETAIL THERAPY

Shopping streets & markets

As Vomero and Capodimonte are residential districts, you would think they would also have an abundance of shopping. But Naples follows centuries-old traditions. For a Neapolitan, shopping means a stroll through the Centro Storico, the markets at La Pignasecca or the boutiques of Chiaia.

Via Scarlatti in Vomero provides the best options. A popular place for a wander, its pedestrianised centre is a great place to people-watch. Shops tend to focus more on household goods and basic needs in these quarters. Exceptions include bookstores and music shops catering to local intellectuals.

FNAC Branch of the French book chain. A limited number of books in English are stocked in case you need some holiday reading. Cinema and concert tickets are also available for purchase. ⓐ Via Luca Giordano 59 ❶ 081 220 1000 Ⓦ www.fnac.it Ⓝ Funicular: Chiaia to via Cimarosa, Centrale to Piazza Fuga; Metro: Vanvitelli

Fonoteca Italy has plenty of bad Eurotrash music – but you won't find any of it in this eclectic music store. A great resource for hard-to-find artists, Fonoteca also boasts great staff and service. Customers are urged to take their time by listening before they make any purchase. ⓐ Via Morghen 31 C/D/E ⓣ 081 556 0338 ⓝ Funicular: Chiaia to via Cimarosa, Centrale to Piazza Fuga; Metro: Vanvitelli; Bus: C36

Studio K Designer furnishings, lamps and household items with a modern flair. ⓐ Via Cimarosa 81 ⓣ 081 556 8240 ⓛ 10.00–13.30, 16.30–20.00 Mon–Sat; closed 3 wks Aug ⓝ Funicular: Chiaia to via Cimarosa, Centrale to Piazza Fuga; Bus: C36

TAKING A BREAK

Bellavia ❶ Naples' best *pasticceria* churns out cakes and cookies by the hundreds. For a real local treat, try the traditional cake made from ricotta cheese. ⓐ Via L Giordano 158 ⓣ 081 578 9684 ⓛ 08.00–21.00 Tues–Sat; closed Aug ⓝ Metro: Collana; Bus: V1

Friggitoria Vomero ❷ On your way to the Castel Sant'Elmo but haven't had breakfast? Stop at this café for doughnuts and coffee. The afternoon brings out the rest of this establishment's fried specialities – including croquettes, courgettes and aubergines in batter. ⓐ Via Domenico Cimarosa 44 ⓣ 081 578 3130 ⓛ 09.30–14.00, 17.00–21.30 Mon–Sat; closed Aug ⓝ Funicular: Centrale to Piazza Fuga or Chiaia to via Cimarosa; Bus: C28, C31, C32, V1

Otranto ❸ Deliciously creamy *gelato* (ice cream) that manages to create queues – even in the winter! What the place lacks in atmosphere, it makes up for in pure yumminess. ⓐ Via Scarlatti 78 ⓣ 081 558 7498 ⓛ 10.00–23.00 Mon, Tues, Thur–Sun May–Sept; 10.00–22.00 Mon, Tues, Thur–Sun Oct–Apr ⓜ Metro: Vanvitelli; Bus: V1

Pizzeria Cilea ❹ If you're on a diet, then avoid the delicious *frittura*. One taste will have you return to the days when deep-fat fryers were all the rage. Be prepared to queue; the *pizzeria* is tiny and extremely popular. If you're in a large group, try somewhere else – slow service could have members in your party waiting for hours. ⓐ Via Cilea 43 ⓣ 081 556 3291 ⓛ 13.00–16.00, 19.30–23.00 Mon–Sat, 07.30–23.30 Sun; closed 2 wks Aug ⓜ Bus: 181, C31, C32

Rosso Pomodoro ❺ For a leisurely slice of pizza, pull up a chair at one of the outdoor tables at this *pizzeria* opposite the Villa Floridiana. Prices are slightly more expensive than other locales, but the free newspapers and comfortable bar make up for the cost difference. ⓐ Via Domenico Cimarosa 144 ⓣ 081 556 8169 ⓛ 13.00–15.00, 19.30–23.00 Mon–Sat; closed Aug ⓜ Funicular: Centrale to Piazza Fuga or Chiaia to via Cimarosa; Bus: C28, C31, C32, V1

AFTER DARK

Restaurants

L'Osteria del Balconcino £ ❻ Popular at lunchtime with local workers, this buzzy *osterie* draws in the masses due to its delicious, no-frills food and rapid service. Don't go here if a 'special' meal is what you have in mind. Instead, use it as a refuelling stop if you happen to be in the neighbourhood. ⓐ Via F Solimene 73 ⓣ 081 229 2213 ⓛ 13.00–15.00, 20.00–24.00 Tues–Sat; 13.00–15.00 Mon, Sun;

closed 2 wks Aug 🅝 Funicular: Chiaia to via Cimarosa or funicular
Centrale to Piazza Fuga; Bus: C28, C31, C32

Osteria Donna Teresa £ 🄿 Dining here is like dining with family. Don't
even think about trying to leave in a rush, as the owner won't let you
go until you finish every bite of two full courses. Don't worry though, as
the delicious traditional dishes will make you want to stay. The local red
wine is the best house option. 🄰 Via Kerbaker 58 🄣 081 556 7070
🄲 12.30–15.00, 19.30–23.00 Mon–Sat; closed Aug 🅝 Funicular: Chiaia to
via Cimarosa or Centrale to Piazza Fuga; Bus: C28, C31, C32

La Cantina di Sica £–££ 🄾 Good for hearty traditional food, the
Cantina di Sica excels with its pasta dishes. Prices are slightly higher
than you might find at other *trattoria* – but you get what you pay
for. Some nights you'll find Neapolitan folk musicians playing in the
wine bar. 🄰 Via Bernini 17 🄣 081 556 7520 🄲 12.30–16.00,
20.00–24.00 Mon, Wed–Sun; closed 1 wk Aug 🅝 Funicular: Chiaia to
via Cimarosa, Centrale to Piazza Fuga; Bus: C28, C31, C32, V1

Il Giardino del Pontano ££ 🄿 Via Scarlatti is the heart of Vomero,
essentially cutting the district in two. This cosy eatery, just off the
pedestrianised main drag, is a real find for a casual evening. A little
courtyard with a garden holds a few tables for al fresco dining.
Occasional theme evenings based on the tastes of specific Italian
regions are sometimes held. Due to its popularity with locals,
advance booking is advised. 🄰 Via Luca Giordano 99 🄣 081 658 4699
🄲 13.00–15.00, 20.00–24.00 Tues–Sun; closed 2 wks Aug
🅝 Funicular: Chiaia to via Cimarosa, Centrale to Piazza Fuga; Bus:
C28, C31, C32, V1

🄾 *A relaxing catch-up*

D'Angelo Santa Caterina ££–£££ ⑩   A dreamy eatery set amid
stunning gardens with inspiring views of the city. For a romantic
meal, this is the place to go. Service is good, if a bit distant. The
seafood antipasti are particularly tasty. ⓐ Via Aniello Falcone 203
ⓣ 081 578 9772 ⓛ 07.30–22.30 Mon, Wed–Sat, 13.00–15.30 Sun;
closed 2 wks Aug ⓝ Bus: C28

Bars, clubs & discos
Around 24.00 Local and national jazz combos play at this dedicated
jazz venue. Go early to snag a seat, as the place is minuscule.
Patrons are extremely friendly. It's a great place to make new
friends with fellow jazz lovers as conversations are always easy to
start up. ⓐ Via Bonito 32A ⓣ 081 558 2834 ⓦ www.around24.00.it
ⓛ 20.30–01.00 Tues–Sun; closed Aug ⓝ Funicular: Montesanto to
San Martino; Metro: Vanvitelli; Bus: V1

Bocca d'Oro Technically a restaurant, this popular Vomero rest-stop
is a good place to start an evening mainly because of its extensive
wine list. Stocked with local vintages, it's a great place to try out
the region's wines. ⓐ Piazzetta Durante 1 ⓣ 081 229 2010
ⓛ 12.30–16.00, 20.30–02.00 Tues–Sat, 20.30–24.00 Mon, Sun; closed
Aug ⓝ Funicular: Chiaia to via Cimarosa or Centrale to
Piazza Fuga; Bus: C28, C31, C32

Cinemas & theatres
Plaza Standard movie theatre that shows English-language features
on Tuesday evenings. ⓐ Via Kerbaker 85 ⓣ 081 556 3555 ⓝ Metro:
Vanvitelli

---

❶ *Head out from the Stazione Circumvesuviana*

OUT OF TOWN
trips

TRENI IN PARTENZA

DEPARTURES

ER ABFAHRT

07.53

DÉPARTS
TRENES E

	CAT.	ORARIO	BIN.		DESTINAZIONE
	ACC	07.48	11		SORRENTO
	ACC	07.54	8		POGGIOMARINO
CAFATI	ACC	08.00	3		POGGIOREALE
DIREZ	ACC	08.02	10		SARNO
TAV	ACC	08.11	5		SORRENTO
IREZ	ACC	08.11	6		SAN GIORGIO
PEI)	DD	08.11			TORRE DEL
	ACC	08.15			BAIANO
	ACC	08.18			

OUT OF TOWN

Herculaneum, Vesuvius & Pompeii

Many say that the purpose of a trip to Naples is not to visit the city itself, but to see everything that surrounds it. No attractions back up this claim more than the excavated remains of the towns of Herculaneum (Ercolano) and Pompeii, destroyed by a massive eruption of Vesuvius in AD 79.

Today these remains are the most visited attractions on the Campanian coastline – and justifiably so. The riches that must have been contained in these popular Roman getaway communities must have been immense judging by the frescoes and artefacts that have been uncovered since the days when the Bourbons began digging up the area. While many of the most priceless treasures have been carted off to the Museo Nazionale in Naples, you can still get a strong idea of what Roman life must have been like simply by looking at the remaining structures.

Despite the constant eruptions, Herculaneum rebuilt itself and is now one of the most densely populated towns in Europe. Much of the Ercolano site remains uncovered due to the volume of humanity that lives above. Who knows what treasures lie beneath?

SIGHTS & ATTRACTIONS: HERCULANEUM

It could be argued that the treasures of Herculaneum are even greater than the remains of Pompeii. What gives this site its secondary status is the fact that much of it exists buried under the existing city of concrete and precarious tower blocks.

Most residents were killed when a shift in the winds and heavy rainfall transformed the earth into a sea of mud, lava and ash that hurtled down on top of the city. When the devastation stopped,

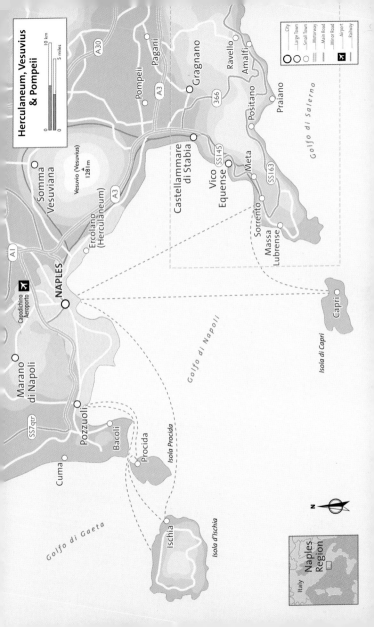

Herculaneum, Vesuvius & Pompeii

City

Large Town

Small Town

Motorway

Main Road

Minor Road

Airport

Railway

10 km

5 miles

A30

Pagani

Gragnano

Ravello

Amalfi

Pompeii

A3

Positano

366

Praiano

A3

Castellammare di Stabia

SS145

Vico Equense

Meta

SS163

Golfo di Salerno

Vesuvio (Vesuvius)
1281m

Somma Vesuviana

Ercolano (Herculāneum)

Sorrento

Massa Lubrense

A1

NAPLES

Capodichino Aeroporto

Capri

Marano di Napoli

Isola di Capri

SS7qtr

Golfo di Napoli

Pozzuoli

Bacoli

Procida

Isola Procida

Cuma

N

Ischia

Isola d'Ischia

Golfo di Gaeta

Italy

Naples Region

the ground level had risen by over 20 m (65 ft), obliterating the entire city from sight.

Archaeologists were both hindered and helped by this volume of mud. Digging through 20 m (65 ft) of earth under a heavily populated city is extremely challenging. Luckily, the mud also served to protect the ancient structures and all the buildings are in a better state of preservation than those at Pompeii.

Scavi di Ercolano

When visiting Herculaneum, it is best to go straight to the site from the Circumvesuviana train line, which is the most common way to get here. The modern town of Ercolano is best avoided. It's one of the region's poorest and there is little of interest other than the Roman excavations to warrant your interest.

Legends say that Herculaneum was founded by Hercules during his return from Iberia. Even though only a small section of the town has been excavated, what has been dug up reveals that Herculaneum was a centre of great importance to the Roman

DOORS TO THE PAST

Limited funds to preserve Herculaneum mean that many of the excavated rooms remain closed to the public. The list of buildings open on a given day is always posted at the ticket office on the Corso Regina. Don't let this stop you from seeing what you want. Get chummy with one of the local guards and you will soon see that a polite smile (and a well-placed euro or two) will uncover even more of the secrets of Herculaneum.

◀ *Vesuvius dominates the landscape and the lives of its inhabitants*

Empire. Luxurious residences stood on the promontory and the lack of any wheel ruts in the paving stones indicates that there wasn't much passing trade. As such, it is believed that the area was reserved for the mega-wealthy who chose to live here in order to enjoy the beauty and tranquillity of the region.

ⓐ Corso Regina 6 ⓣ 081 739 0963 ⓛ 08.30–19.30 Apr–Oct, ticket office closes 18.00; 08.30–17.00 Nov–Mar, ticket office closes 15.30 ⓝ Circumvesuviana railway to Ercolano (Herculaneum)

SIGHTS & ATTRACTIONS: MOUNT VESUVIUS

Naples – just like the rest of Campania – lives and dies by the moans and mutterings of Mount Vesuvius. One might think that the residents of one of Europe's most densely populated regions would be mad for choosing to live next to an active volcano, and you would be correct. The most recent volcanic eruption occurred in 1944. Evidence of the lava flow from that explosion is still visible close to the remains at Pompeii – and that's not taking into account the earthquakes that often occur in volcanic regions. Scientists often say that the 'big one' is right around the corner.

So why do the locals stay? The main reason is agriculture. Campanian soil is extraordinarily rich in nutrients. Crops flourish remarkably well in the region and local produce is considered top-notch. That combined with a gorgeous climate, incredible topography, beautiful islands and waters stocked with seafood translate into a glorious lifestyle.

Cratere del Vesuvio

Vesuvius may look calm at a distance, but a hike up close reveals the truth. This deceptive peak has killed thousands and continues to worry the experts of the Osseratorio Vesuviano, the institute that has been monitoring the volcano's activity ever since 1841.

A walk up the peak is a popular pastime and well worth considering even if you aren't a regular hiker. Declared a UNESCO Biosphere Reserve, the volcano is a protected plot of land attracting 200,000 visitors each year. Hiking is permitted right to the rim of the cone, allowing visitors the opportunity to peek into the depths of the crater 200 m (650 ft) below.

A hike up the mountain works best in May and early June when mornings tend to be calm and clear. Setting off on a windy day is not advised, as conditions can be challenging.

A standard 30-minute route takes visitors from the car park to the rim along a well-maintained path. The car park is located at the end of the road on the volcano's west side. A funicular railway built by the same team behind the funiculars leading up to the Vomero neighbourhood in Naples used to provide a comfortable option. However, it was destroyed during the eruption of 1944.

The most intriguing structure is a museum and observatory chronicling the volcano's history – but not for the displays. What most fascinates is the question of how the Bourbon-era building has managed to survive at least seven eruptions without a sign of damage!

ⓐ Cratere del Vesuvio ❶ 081 777 5720 ⏰ 09.00–2 hrs before sunset
Ⓜ Transporti Vesuviani from the Piazza Anfiteatro in Pompeii or Ercolano station

SIGHTS & ATTRACTIONS: POMPEII

Pompeii was immortalised on 24 August AD 79 when Vesuvius erupted in a sea of lava, ash and sulphurous gases. Residents initially thought they were out of firing range and many stayed to weather the storm. A rapidly moving, super-heated cloud of gases made them regret this decision, killing many as they huddled in their homes. The cloud occurred so suddenly that, when archaeologists dug up Pompeii centuries later, they were able to make plaster casts from the spaces formed by bodies that had long since disintegrated. Several were performing everyday tasks, causing many to believe that the cloud must have overcome people almost instantly.

By the time of the eruption, Pompeii was a city in decline. While it was still a favoured playground for the rich of the Roman Empire, its status was far from the glory days of a mere two centuries earlier when its importance rivalled even Naples.

Pompeii owed its popularity to its strategic position near the Sarno River. Buildings were developed using Greek techniques, resulting in a well-ordered grid pattern. Roads were paved from slabs of old lava, while the villas and houses of the rich and powerful were constructed from stone, brick and cement – many highly decorated.

Streets, workshops and public areas are in a wonderful state of preservation, and there is much more to uncover. Recent roadworks on the Naples–Salerno motorway revealed a frescoed leisure complex. Treasures such as jewellery, tools, furnishings and even preserved food and drink have provided key insights into how the Romans lived – both as slaves and as citizens.

One of Pompeii's many victims

CULTURE

Scavi di Pompeii

The ruins at Pompeii are one of the most visited sights in all of Italy and have been almost since the day they were uncovered in 1750. Historians of the day unearthed the site using techniques that would make modern-day archaeologists shudder in horror. Along with the bodies of the dead, treasures including magnificent frescoes, temples and everyday objects were dug up and shipped to the Museo Nazionale.

Today, the ruins look a little the worse for wear. While still well-maintained, the sheer volume of visitors is having its effect. Audioguides haven't been updated in years, many major structures are closed for parts of the day and touts have been given free access to hassle for business. There are no limits on the number of visitors who can enter on a daily basis, meaning public holidays and weekends are often packed. It's hard to imagine the rise and fall of the Roman Empire when you've got a baby screaming in your ear, a chain-smoking tourist stubbing out cigarettes on the stone floor and backpackers stopping immediately in front of you to photograph every fresco.

The most important structures to view are the great houses concentrated along the Via dell'Abbondanza and between the Via del Mercurio in the northwest of Pompeii and Via Stabiana. The homes of the wealthiest residents are easily spotted as they feature courtyards, living rooms and – the most prized possession of all – private gardens. A typical home is focused around two open courts, each featuring elements of Greek and Italian architecture.

When visiting Pompeii, it is best to bring plenty of water and wear appropriate headwear. There is very little shade available anywhere on-site and crowds can get claustrophobic. To truly avoid the bulk of visitors, go later in the day when tour buses are long gone.

ⓐ Via Villa dei Mistri 2 ☎ 081 857 5347 ⏰ 08.30–19.30, ticket office closes 18.00, Apr–Oct; 08.30–17.00, ticket office closes 15.30, Nov–Mar ⓜ Circumvesuviana to Pompeii Stavi – Villa dei Misteri

Suggestioni al Foro

Touring the ruins of Pompeii after dark is a possibility thanks to a new tour that takes a limited number of travellers through the civic and religious buildings that surround the main square. While the number of rooms on view is small, seeing everything accompanied by a few torches and some 'arty' lighting enhances the experience of seeing the ruins – especially as you aren't surrounded by hundreds of package tourists.

☎ 347 346 0346 ⏰ Tours in English are offered at 20.30 Wed Nov–Mar, 21.30 Wed Apr–Oct

🔺 Sample some star-quality seafood

AFTER DARK

Restaurants

Il Principe £££ This restaurant is one of Campania's finest. Dishes are all drawn from history, including recipes from ancient authors. The result is an unusual variety of ingredients and flavours. ➋ Piazza B Longo 8 ❶ 081 850 5566 ❺ 12.30–15.30, 19.00–23.30 Tues–Sat, 12.30–15.30 Sun, Mon, Apr–Oct; 12.30–15.30, 19.00–23.30 Tues–Sat, 12.30–15.30 Sun, Nov–Mar; closed 3 wks Aug ❻ Circumvesuviana to Pompeii Stavi – Villa dei Misteri

ACCOMMODATION

Casa del Pellegrino £ A well-placed hostel offering both dorms and private family rooms in a converted convent. Furnishings are basic. ➋ Via Duca D'Aosta 4 ❶ 081 850 8644 ❽ www.hostels-aig.org ❻ Circumvesuviana to Pompeii Stavi – Villa dei Misteri

PROFITS OF DOOM

Residents of Campania are familiar with natural disasters, but they also know how to turn a profit once the dust has cleared. Locals are still coping with the effects of the 1980 earthquake, which killed thousands. Even worse, though, was the mass corruption that sucked millions from the coffers of the regional government as unscrupulous developers built shoddy, unregulated tower blocks up and down the coast. This phenomena is not new. Emperor Vespasian noticed the same problems when he sent a tribune to enforce zoning laws following the earthquake of AD 62.

Hotel Amleto ££ This quaint property is located steps away from the entrance to the archaeological zone. Rooms are themed in a variety of 'old' Italian styles, some featuring attractive *trompe l'oeil* wall paintings. ❸ Via B Longo 10 ❶ 081 863 1004 ❿ www.hotelamleto.it ❿ Circumvesuviana to Pompeii Stavi – Villa dei Misteri

🔺 *Fresco from a house in Pompeii*

The Amalfi Coast

The Amalfi Coast is one of nature's wonders. Rocky cliffs plunge into the Mediterranean dotted with pastel-hued towns that precariously cling to the peninsula. The visuals would inspire anyone – and often have. Authors as diverse as Steinbeck, Shelley, Byron and Goethe have explored the region and marvelled over its beauty.

That said, living here hasn't always been so delightful. Until roads were carved out of the cliffs, residents were cut off from the rest of Italy and subject to constant pirate raids and storms.

Today, the attacks come in the form of crowds of tourists and massive tour buses that clog the roads every summer weekend. If you are planning a drive along the coast – and it is surely one of the world's most beautiful driving itineraries – avoid a trip during the weekend when the coast road turns into a massive parking lot.

The traditional drive begins in Sorrento and follows the 145 until Amalfi. Some intrepid travellers continue the journey to Ravello if they have the time. If you are a nervous driver, consider booking yourself on a tour. While you won't have the same flexibility, the road has enough hairpin turns to make even Schumacher fearful. Be very careful when passing as the road is barely big enough for one car, let alone two. Above all, the key to enjoyment is stopping. Don't get sucked into the monotony of the drive, for it is the exploration of the individual towns along the way that will provide the most memorable moments.

SORRENTO

A favourite with British tourists ever since the days of the 'grand tour', Sorrento is the gateway to the Sorrentine Peninsula and a popular starting point for the famed drive along the Amalfi Coast.

It may seem that package tourists have over-run the place, but it's easy to escape the English pubs and blue-rinse brigade to discover the magic that brought all these people here in the first place.

SIGHTS & ATTRACTIONS

Duomo

The original cathedral of Sorrento was rebuilt in the Gothic style. Fine examples of local *intarsio* (wooden inlay) work decorate the choir stalls. Of particular note is the bishop's throne dating from 1573 constructed from marble fragments.

ⓐ Corso Italia ⓣ 081 878 2248 ⓛ 07.40–12.00, 16.30–20.30

CULTURE

Museobottega della Tarsialignea

This museum, situated in a restored 18th-century *palazzo*, displays the best of local handicraft and artwork including stunning examples of wooden inlay furniture. Old paintings and photographs of Sorrento provide additional context.

ⓐ Via San Nicola 28 ⓣ 081 877 1942
ⓦ www.alessandrofiroentinocollection.it ⓛ 09.30–13.00, 16.00–20.00 Tues–Sun Apr–Oct; 09.30–13.00, 15.00–19.00 Tues–Sun Nov–Mar

Museo Correale di Terranova

A jumbled collection of local art and artefacts left to the town by two brothers in the 1920s. The archaeological section boasts the

ⓞ *A lively corner of Sorrento's Piazza Tasso*

best exhibits, including a collection of Greek and Roman marbles, Greek classical sculptures and vases. There are also minor works of the 17th and 18th centuries from the Neapolitan school of painters and artists.

ⓐ Via Correale 50 ⓣ 081 878 1846 ⓛ 09.00–14.00 Mon, Wed–Sun

RETAIL THERAPY

Primo Piano Oggetti Original ceramic tiles, plates and cups. ⓐ Corso Italia 161 ⓣ 081 807 2927 ⓛ 09.00–13.30, 16.30–20.00 Tues–Sat

Salvatore Gargiulo Sorrento's best furniture workshop specialising in marquetry and wooden inlay. ⓐ Via Fuoro 33 ⓣ 081 878 2420 ⓦ www.gargiuloinlaid.it ⓛ 09.30–13.00, 16.00–19.00 Tues–Sun

TAKING A BREAK

Bar Ercolano Lovely outdoor café perfect for people-watching. Service is slow, but the quality of the ice cream compensates. ⓐ Piazza Tasso ⓣ 081 807 2951 ⓛ 06.00–01.30 Mon, Wed–Sun Apr–Sept; 06.00–22.30 Mon, Wed–Sun Oct–Mar

Il Fauno Of all the cafés in the centre of Sorrento, this is the chicest. The high end of society wouldn't be caught anywhere else. People-watching possibilities are delicious. You won't mind the higher-than-average prices, as the service and range of beverages are superb. ⓐ Piazza Tasso 13–15 ⓣ 081 878 7735 ⓦ www.faunobar.it ⓛ 07.00–24.00

AFTER DARK

Restaurants

Da Emilia £ Unassuming family-run restaurant with friendly service and traditional, hearty cuisine. Grab a chair at one of the wooden tables and enjoy. ⓐ Via Marina Grande 62 ⓣ 081 807 2720 ⓛ 12.30–15.00, 19.30–23.30 July, Aug; 12.30–15.00, 19.00–23.30 Mon, Wed–Sun Apr–June, Sept, Oct; intermittent lunches Nov–Mar

Ristorante Vittoria ££ Step back in time and imagine the days when a 'grand tour' through Italy was a must for any debutante and dandy worth their salt. White-jacketed waiters put on a formal display of 'old school' service. Dishes are hit and miss, but it's the atmosphere and inspiringly frescoed dining room that continues to draw the crowds. ⓐ Grand Hotel Excelsior Vittoria, Piazza Tasso 34 ⓣ 081 807 1044 ⓛ 12.30–14.00, 19.30–22.30

Cinemas & theatres

Estate Musicale Sorrentina Sorrento's summer season of live performances. Most concerts are free of charge and good quality. Check listings on the website. ⓦ www.estatemusicalesorrentina.it

ACCOMMODATION

Ostello delle Sirene (Youth Hostel) £ If your budget can't quite afford 5-star luxury but you still want to stay in Sorrento, check into the youth hostel. The accommodation is basic but they're the cheapest beds in town. ⓐ Via degli Aranci 160 ⓣ 081 807 2925

Imperial Hotel Tramontano £££ There are many 5-star properties in
Naples, but this is my pick for a truly special holiday. Shelley, Byron,
Goethe and Ibsen all enjoyed this hotel. Its cliff-side location,
beautiful pool and private beach will do much to help convince
you that they were right. ⓐ Via Veneto 1 ⓣ 081 878 2588
ⓦ www.tramontano.com

🔺 *The stunning seaside town of Positano*

POSITANO

Probably the Amalfi Coast's most visually stunning town, Positano is a precariously perched community that found its place on the tourist map in the 1950s following years of decline. During the 18th and 19th centuries, many locals emigrated, unable to continue facing the harsh conditions, pirate attacks and being detached from the rest of the country. When roads finally opened up the region to the outside world, the outside world moved in to take advantage of the glorious lifestyle this 'cliff with houses on it' had to offer.

RETAIL THERAPY

La Libreria This bookshop fits the bill if you need some holiday reading material. The English language selection is limited but there is a nice range of local guidebooks if you need further inspiration. ⓐ Via Columbo 165 ⓣ 089 811 077 ⓛ 11.30–15.00, 16.00–19.00 Tues–Sat; closed mid-Nov–Feb

AFTER DARK

Restaurants

Donna Rosa ££ This elegant *trattoria* boasting views over the main village is an extremely romantic spot for a meal. For summer evenings, you must book a table at least a day in advance to ensure availability. Lunches tend to be quieter and therefore a better option if you're travelling at the last minute. ⓐ Via Montepertuso 97/99 ⓣ 089 811 806 ⓛ 19.00–23.30 Aug; 19.00–23.00 Mon, Tues, 12.00–16.00, 19.00–23.00 Wed–Sun, May–July, Sept, Oct; 12.00–16.00, 19.00–23.00 Mon, Wed–Sun Apr, Nov, Dec; closed Jan–Mar

Il Capitano £££ Locals and holidaymakers agree that Il Capitano is Positano's best restaurant. Dishes are classic and delicious. Fish dishes are especially recommended. The views of the coast from the terrace are superb. If you want an outside table, book well in advance. ⓐ Via Pasitea 119 ⓣ 089 811 351 ⓦ www.hotelmontemare.it ⓛ 12.00–15.00, 19.00–22.30 Mon, Tues, Thur–Sun; 19.30–22.30 Wed; closed Nov–Apr

Clubs & bars
Africana Hidden in a rocky cove, this amazing dance club features a dance floor inside a grotto. Youth from across the Sorrentine Peninsula make a beeline for this hotspot, especially in summer when direct boats run to and from Salerno, Maiori, Minori and Amalfi. ⓐ West of Marina di Praia, between Positano and Amalfi ⓣ 089 874 042 ⓛ 22.30–04.00 Wed–Sun; closed Oct–May

ACCOMMODATION

Maria Luisa ££ This hotel is the cheapest one in town. You don't get any frills, but the rooms are clean, bright and sea-facing. For a little extra, it's possible to get a panoramic balcony. A nice option if you want a Positano address but are on a budget. ⓐ Via Fornillo 42 ⓣ 089 875 023

San Pietro £££ The San Pietro could have strong arguments for being the most luxurious and exclusive hotel in all of Italy. Constructed from a private villa just 2 km (1.2 miles) east of Positano, the property is extremely private – the only way people know it exists is by a tiny sign by the side of the road. Rooms feature Jacuzzis and private balconies. A lift takes guests down to the private beach. Worth the (major) splurge. ⓐ Via Laurito 2 ⓣ 089 875 455 ⓦ www.ilsanpietro.it

AMALFI

The Amalfi Coast gets its name from this beautiful town, which seems to cling to the rockface it sits on. Once a powerful maritime republic, the area boomed during the 11th century when it was one of Italy's richest cities – rivalling Venice and Genoa in trade volume and traffic.

Amalfi sailors were – and still are – respected. For many years, the bulk of residents made their fortunes renting themselves out as marine mercenaries terrorising the high seas. Little evidence of the days when Amalfi boasted a population of 60,000 remain. What is left, however, is a joy to wander through and savour.

SIGHTS & ATTRACTIONS

Duomo di Amalfi

Amalfi's main cathedral was founded in the 9th century and has been rebuilt many times. The structure is a combination of styles ranging from Italian Romanesque to neoclassical. Surprisingly the mish-mash works. The only part of the church that has survived since its original construction is the Cappella del Crocefisso, which holds the major treasures of the church including a 15th-century bas relief and a bejewelled mitre. ⓐ Piazza del Duomo ⓣ 089 871 059 ⓛ 09.00–19.00 Apr–June; 09.00–21.00 July–Sept; 09.30–17.00 Oct, Mar; 10.00–13.00, 14.30–16.30 Nov–Feb

CULTURE

Museo della Carta

The valley that surrounds Amalfi was known for centuries as the
site of some of Europe's leading paper manufacturers. One of the
original factories has now been transformed into a museum
illustrating the history and techniques of the trade.
ⓐ Via delle Cartiere 23 ⓣ 089 830 4561 ⓦ www.museodellacarta.it
ⓛ 10.00–15.00 Tues–Sun Nov–Mar; 10.00–18.00 Apr–June, Oct;
10.00–20.00 July–Sept

RETAIL THERAPY

Antichi Sapori d'Amalfi Delightful selection of homemade
limoncello and fruit liquors. ⓐ Piazza del Duomo 39 ⓣ 089 872 062
ⓛ 11.00–15.30, 16.00–19.30 Mon–Wed, Fri, Sat, 11.00–15.30 Sun

La Scuderia del Duca Purchase some beautiful handmade paper or
choose from a selection of books on Amalfi from this delightfully
old-fashioned stationers. ⓐ Largo Cesareo Console 8 ⓣ 089 872 976
ⓦ www.carta-amalfi.it ⓛ 11.00–15.30, 16.30–19.00 Tues–Sat

AFTER DARK

Restaurants
La Caravella £££ The fact that this restaurant is always full should
give you a good clue that it is considered Amalfi's best restaurant.
Despite the fact that the views are uninspiring (there aren't any),

⓿ *Take time out on the beach at Amalfi*

the seafood, service and wine list will convince any doubters of its superiority. Seafood is a highlight. The kitchen does wonders with the catch of the day. Desserts are less successful. ❸ Via Matteo Camera 12 ❶ 089 871 029 ⓦ www.ristorantelacaravella.it ❶ 12.00–14.30, 19.30–22.30 Mon, Wed–Sun; closed mid-Nov–Dec

Da Maria £–££ Your head will spin at the sheer number of cheap *pizzeria* and *trattoria* who have set up business in Amalfi.

⬤ *Amalfi's cathedral is a wonderful mish-mash of styles*

Da Maria features the same menu and prices as the rest, but the food is somehow a touch better than the average rest-stop. The seafood pastas and pizzas are especially good. ❸ Via Lorenzo d'Amalfi 14 ❶ 089 871 880 ❷ 12.00–15.00, 19.30–22.30 Tues–Sun; closed Nov

Bars & clubs
Bar Risacca Local favourite hangout. A favoured place for breakfast by day or a Campari and soda by night. ❸ Piazza Umberto I 16 ❶ 089 872 866 ❷ 09.00–15.00, 19.00–24.00 Apr–Oct; 09.00–15.00, 19.00–24.00 Tues–Sun Nov–Mar

RoccoCò Cheesy nightclub featuring bad Eurotrash music and even worse DJs. Think 'wedding from hell' and you get the idea. Good if you're in need of a boogie and don't care who sees you. ❸ Via delle Cartiere 98 ❶ 089 873 080 ❷ 22.00–03.00 Apr–Oct; 22.00–03.00 Fri, Sat Nov–Mar

ACCOMMODATION

Amalfi £–££ This quality 3-star is the town's best moderate option. Service is efficient, but the property can sometimes feel like it is over-run by British tour groups. ❸ Vico dei Pastai 3 ❶ 089 872 440 ⓦ www.hamalfi.it ❷ Closed mid-Jan–Feb

Santa Caterina £££ The Santa Caterina is a stunning 5-star property located just west of Amalfi towards Positano. The hotel has a stretch of private beach all to itself – but you may not even step on it as you can enjoy the sun's rays from the comfort of your private terrace. ❸ Via Nazionale 9 ❶ 089 871 012 ⓦ www.hotelsantacaterina.it

Capri, Ischia & Procida

The islands of Capri, Ischia and Procida are stunning. Sleepy during the winter months – you probably won't find anyone except for a few diehard natives and a couple of cats anywhere in January or February – the islands positively boom the minute the sun starts to heat their pebbly beaches.

Each island has its own characteristics and fans. Capri, with its designer boutiques and range of extortionate hotels, appeals to new-money and youthful exuberance. Ischia is more for the established old-money set and those looking for quiet, calm and relaxation. Finally, there's Procida – a jewel of an island made for sleepy days in the sun and quiet meals under the stars.

Reaching the islands during the summer couldn't be easier. Ferries and hydrofoils leave regularly from the Molo Beverello in Naples. There are also frequent services from Mergellina, Pozzuoli, Sorrento and Positano.

CAPRI

The brashest of Campania's holiday islands, Capri has been a favourite of artists for centuries. Everyone from the Roman Emperor Tiberius to W H Auden has been entranced by the island's topography, especially its famed Blue Grotto. Tiberius was so

> ❶ Be sure to book well in advance if you want to visit these areas during high season, as hotel rooms and restaurants fill up fast, especially in August.

❶ *Heading out to the Blue Grotto*

bewitched by Capri that he temporarily moved the capital of the Roman Empire to its shores.

Today, Capri is best known as a millionaires' playground complete with high-end designer boutiques, swish cafés serving €5 cups of coffee and exclusive resorts.

Due to space limitations, recommendations in this section will be limited to the offerings close to Capri Town. For more detailed descriptions of Anacapri and the rest of the island, please refer to *Travellers' Naples & Amalfi Coast* – another title in the Thomas Cook Publishing range of guidebooks.

SIGHTS & ATTRACTIONS

Grotta Azzura (Blue Grotto)

If there is one sight to see on Capri, then this is it. The mysterious blue hue is created by refraction of the light. The colour has inspired more than a few artists, especially during the 19th century when various poets raved about its mystical qualities. Tours can be arranged at the Marina Grande and last about an hour in duration.

🕐 09.00–1 hr before sunset

RETAIL THERAPY

Limoncello di Capri The first and original. This boutique created the famous lemon liquor now available all across Campania. This is the place to buy a bottle. Drink it straight or on ice – but always chilled. ❸ Via Roma 79 ☎ 081 837 5561
🔾 www.limoncello.com 🕐 11.00–19.30 Apr–Oct; 11.00–14.30, 17.00–19.30 Tues–Sun Nov–Mar

TAKING A BREAK

Piccolo Bar There are four major bars on the Piazzetta – and there are very few differences between them. This establishment is the oldest on the square and offers great people-watching perches. ⓐ Piazzetta ⓣ 081 837 0325 ⓛ 09.00–23.00 Apr–Oct; 09.00–23.00 Tues–Sun Nov–Mar

AFTER DARK

Restaurants
La Capannina £££ This romantic, family-run establishment continues to draw the high and mighty of Capri. Don't go if you're looking for something experimental; this place has been serving its classic versions of traditional cuisine since it opened back in the 1930s. ⓐ Via Le Botteghe 12 bis ⓣ 081 837 0732 ⓛ 12.00–14.00, 19.30–24.00 May–Sept; 12.00–14.00, 19.30–24.00 Mon, Tues, Thur–Sun mid-Mar, Apr, Oct, 1st wk Nov; closed 2nd wk Nov–mid-Mar

Villa Verde £££ Where the stars come out to eat. Traditional caprese food is this restaurant's speciality – and boy does it do it well. Despite the simple furnishings, this place is one of the most expensive in Capri. ⓐ Vico Sella Orta 6A ⓣ 081 837 7024 ⓦ www.villaverdecapri.com ⓛ 12.00–15.30, 19.30–24.00 Apr–Oct; 12.00–15.30, 19.30–24.00 Tues–Sun Nov–Mar

Cinemas & theatres
Auditorium The main cinema for Capri town. Screenings are usually dubbed and have a leaning towards Hollywood blockbusters. ⓐ Vico Sella Orta 3 ⓣ 081 837 6926 ⓛ closed Mon, Thur, Fri Oct–Apr

ACCOMMODATION

Villa Sarah ££ Want to stay on Capri but don't have a Swiss bank account? This cheery Mediterranean villa should fit the bill. Expensive for what you get, it's still a bargain when compared to every other hotel in Capri town. ⓐ Via Tiberio 3A ⓣ 081 837 7817 ⓦ www.villasarah.it ⓛ Closed Nov–Mar

Grand Hotel Quisisana £££ A Capri institution. Stay here if you want to mix with celebs and live the high life. Is that Mariah Carey chatting to Prince Albert of Monaco by the pool? Probably. ⓐ Via Camerelle 2 ⓣ 081 837 0788 ⓦ www.quisi.com ⓛ Closed Nov–mid-Mar

ISCHIA

Many people have described Ischia as Capri's less-popular sister. While both are chic and boast amazing panoramas, Ischia is just that little less brash. Capri fans may have all the designer boutiques, but lovers of Ischia don't care. What they lack in designer duds they make up for in the form of natural spas, wider beaches and verdant hills.

The largest of all the islands off the Campanian coastline, Ischia can actually be divided into many regions. Due to space limitations, recommendations in this section will be limited to the offerings close to Ischia Porto. For more detailed descriptions of the island and its sights, please refer to *Travellers' Naples & Amalfi Coast* – another title in the Thomas Cook Publishing range of guidebooks.

ⓞ *Capri's bustling Piazzetta*

SIGHTS & ATTRACTIONS

Castello Aragonese

Originally fortified by the Greeks in the 5th century BC, this rocky outcrop has been used as a stronghold by Romans, Goths, Arabs and the British. The Castello found fame in the 16th century when it became home to the court of Vittoria Colonna, the wife of Ischia's feudal lord, Ferrante d'Avalos.

Attacks during the 18th century forced 2,000 families to move behind its protected walls – and it took over a century before they decided to move back out. During this period 13 churches were built on its grounds.

Of all the attacking forces, it is the British who caused the most damage to the structure. During their bombardment of 1809, they aggressively attempted to remove the French from the island. Evidence of the battles can still be seen in the walls pockmarked by gunshot and shrapnel.

🕾 081 992 834 🕐 09.00–1 hr before sunset Mar–Nov; closed Dec–Feb

La Mortella

Lush, green gardens that house more than 3,000 varieties of plantlife, most of which are extremely rare.

🄰 Via F Calise 35, Forio 🕾 081 986 220 🕸 www.ischia.it/mortella
🕐 09.00–19.00 Tues, Thur, Sat & Sun Apr–mid-Nov

Spas

Terme di Cava Scura Ischia's most naturally beautiful spa, the Terme di Cava Scura is hewn out of rugged cliffs located at the end of one of Ischia's most stunning walking trails. Designed for the truly knowledgeable spa-goer, treatments include massages, facials and thermal baths in divine locations, including a natural cave. ⓐ Via Cava Scura, Spiaggia dei Maronti ⓣ 081 905 564 ⓛ 08.30–13.30, 14.30–18.00 mid-Apr–Oct; closed Nov–mid-Apr

Negombo Public spa open to day visitors. The entrance fee allows access to a stunning garden filled with hundreds of exotic plants, the San Montano beach and the obligatory thermal spa facilities. ⓐ Via Baia di San Montano, Lacco Ameno ⓣ 081 986 152 ⓦ www.negombo.it ⓛ 08.30–19.00; closed mid-Oct–mid-Apr

TAKING A BREAK

Da Ciccio The best ice cream on Ischia. No questions asked. It's almost worth visiting the island just for a scoop. ⓐ Piazza Antica Reggia 5 ⓣ 081 991 314 ⓛ 07.00–24.00 Tues–Sun Nov–Feb; 07.00–02.00 Mar–Oct

Pane & Vino This late-closing shop sells exactly what you think – bread and wine. A great place to stock up for picnic supplies or prior to a ferry journey. The other passengers will be green with envy (or the roll of the waves, depending on what the weather is like). ⓐ Via Porto 24 ⓣ 081 991 046 ⓛ 10.00–13.00, 16.30–21.30 Mon, Tues, Thur–Sun Nov–mid-Jan, Mar; 10.00–02.00 Apr–Oct; closed mid-Jan–Feb

AFTER DARK

Restaurants
Cocò ££ Simple seafood and pasta dishes. The place is often filled with locals. ⓐ Piazzale Aragonese ⓣ 081 981 823 ⓛ 12.30–15.00,

19.30–23.00 Mon, Tues, Thur–Sun Mar, Apr, Oct–Dec; 12.30–15.00, 19.30–23.00 May–Sept; closed Jan, Feb

Alberto a Mare £££ Shell out happily for the dishes at this lovely restaurant that sits on a platform overlooking the sea. It's hard to know which is more inspiring: the sunsets or the food. ⓐ Via Cristoforo Colombo 8 ⓣ 081 981 259 ⓛ 12.00–15.00, 19.00–23.00; closed Nov–mid-Mar

Bars, clubs & discos
Bar Calice The streets around this buzzy bar may turn you off – but if you decide not to go, you'll be missing out on some of the island's best ice cream and cakes. A great place for a late-night coffee and chat. ⓐ Piazza degli Eroi 69 ⓣ 081 991 270 ⓛ 07.00–02.00 Mon, Tues, Thur–Sun Nov–Mar; 07.00–02.00 Apr–Oct

Oh! X Bacco This jolly wine bar serves tasty nibbles. If you're in a larger group, consider ordering the *menu degustazione* which provides a variety of antipasti samples. ⓐ Via Luigi Mazzella 20 ⓣ 081 991 354 ⓛ 18.00–24.00 Mon, Wed, 11.00–15.00, 18.00–24.00 Thur–Sun, Nov–Feb; 11.00–15.00, 19.00–02.00 Mon, Wed–Sun Mar–Oct

ACCOMMODATION

Miramare e Castello £££ Located directly on the beach, the Miramare is a lovely hotel for a relaxing break. Choose from rooms with or without a terrace depending on your budget.

◀ *Drinks with the smart set on Capri*

Spa packages are available. ➋ Via Pontano 9 ➊ 081 991 333
➍ www.miramareecastello.it ➌ Closed mid-Oct–mid-Apr

Il Moresco £££ White Moorish arches and wrought-iron gratings
combine to create this sublime hotel. Lose yourself in the gardens
or take a dip in the thermal pool located in a rocky cave. ➋ Via E
Gianturco 16 ➊ 081 981 355 ➍ www.ilmoresco.it ➌ Closed mid-
Oct–mid-Apr

PROCIDA

The main port of Procida has been in existence almost since the
days the Greeks first explored the region in the 5th century BC.
Today, the architecture is highly influenced by the mini-population
boom of the 17th and 18th centuries when neoclassical looks were
all the rage.

SIGHTS & ATTRACTIONS

Abbazia di San Michele Arcangelo

Dating back to 1026, the abbey has been rebuilt a number of times.
The building has a painting of the archangel Michael by Luca
Giordano, a large manuscript museum, Nativity scene and
labyrinthine catacombs that lead to a secret chapel.
➋ Via Terra Murata 89 ➊ 081 896 7612 ➌ 10.00–12.45, 15.00–18.00
Mon–Sat, 09.45–12.45 Sun

Castello d'Avalos

You may not be able to enter the foreboding walls today, but up
until 1986, you wouldn't have wanted to. Castello d'Avalos was
Italy's answer to Alcatraz – an island prison where only the worst

offenders were sent. The massive structure is the first building you see when arriving at Procida's Marina Grande. As yet, there are no plans to open up the building as a tourist attraction.

TAKING A BREAK

Bar Roma Delicious cakes are what's on offer at this casual bar next to the church of Santa Maria della Pietà. Order a coffee and forget about the diet for a relaxing afternoon. ⓐ Via Roma 163 ① 081 896 7460 ① 12.00–15.00, 19.00–23.00 May–Sept; 12.00–15.00, 19.00–23.00 Mon, Wed–Sun Oct–Apr

Bar del Cavaliere The local bourgeoisie love sipping cocktails at this buzzy bar on the via Roma. The only place on the island that knows how to mix a good drink. ⓐ Via Roma 42–43 ① 081 810 1074 ① 12.30–15.30, 19.00–23.00 Apr–Sept; 12.30–15.30, 19.00–23.00 Tues–Sun Oct–Mar

AFTER DARK

Restaurants

Fammivento £–££ If you want to enjoy the hustle and bustle of the Marina Grande, choose this restaurant for its service with a smile. Portions are enormous; just don't annoy the parrot. ⓐ Via Roma 39 ① 081 896 9020 ① 12.30–15.30, 19.00–23.00 Tues–Sun Mar–June, Sept–Dec; 12.30–15.30, 19.00–23.00 Aug; closed Jan, Feb

La Pergola ££ Advance booking is always recommended at this intriguing and small garden restaurant, which does wonders with local ingredients. The menu changes daily and always features a

wide variety of tasty possibilities. ⓐ Via V Rinaldi 37 ⓣ 081 896 9534
ⓛ 12.30–15.30, 19.00–23.00 Tues–Sun mid-Apr–July, Sept, Oct;
12.30–15.30, 19.00–23.00 Aug; closed Nov–mid-Apr

ACCOMMODATION

La Casa sul Mare ££–£££ This romantic hotel is located in a restored
18th-century *palazzo*. Rooms are air-conditioned and feature
beautiful terraces overlooking the bay. Transfers to Chiaja beach are
available free of charge. ⓐ Sailta Castello 13 ⓣ 081 896 8799
ⓦ www.lacasasulmare.it ⓛ Closed 3 wks Jan, Feb

La Tonnara ££–£££ Families love this property due to its proximity
to a sandy beach. The rooftop and solarium boast stunning views.
ⓐ Via Marina Chiaiolella 51/B ⓣ 081 810 1052

● *Take a ferry to explore the islands*

● *Even the traffic police are stylish*

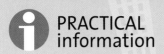

PRACTICAL information

Directory

GETTING THERE

By air

For a short stay, those coming from the UK will find flying the quickest and most convenient way to get to Naples. The main entry point is Capodichino Airport, which is served by most major European airlines and some low-cost services. Travellers from the USA will need to change planes in a European hub before reaching their final destination, as there are no non-stop services from North America. The average flying time from London is 2 hrs, or 8½ hrs from New York including connections. See also page 48 for more details on airports.

By rail

Though travelling by rail is often a more expensive option than flying from the UK, it at least allows you the chance to see something of the countryside en route. Two of the most common routes by rail either cut through France and into Italy via Turin and Rome or cross through Switzerland and into Italy via Milan.

There are fast and comfortable connections using the French routings from London's Waterloo International station with Eurostar. It involves a change in Paris and at Turin. You may also need to change trains at either Milan or Rome depending on which service you travel on. The total journey time is approximately 16–20 hours, depending on connections. The monthly *Thomas Cook European Rail Timetable* has up-to-date schedules for European international and domestic train services.

▶ *The striking central post office building*

Eurostar reservations (UK). ☎ 08705 186 186 ⓦ www.eurostar.com
Thomas Cook European Rail Timetable (UK) ☎ 01733 416 477
(USA) ☎ 1 800 322 3834 ⓦ www.thomascookpublishing.com

Driving

The Italian motorway system is well integrated in the European
motorway network. The easiest motorway to use is the A1, which
cuts through Italy and passes through Rome to terminate at
Naples. The trip from London via Calais, Paris, Nice, Genoa, Florence
and Rome may be picturesque, but it's a long drive at approximately
20 hours.

CUSTOMS

There are no customs controls at borders for visitors from EU
countries. Visitors from EU countries can bring in, or take out,
goods without restrictions on quantity or value, as long as
these goods are for personal use only. For visitors from outside
the EU, most personal effects and the following items are duty
free: a portable typewriter, one video camera or two still
cameras with 10 rolls of film each, a portable radio, a tape
recorder and a laptop computer provided they show signs of
use; 400 cigarettes **or** 50 cigars **or** 250 g of tobacco; 2 litres of
wine **or** 1 litre of liquor per person over 17 years old; fishing
gear; one bicycle; skis; tennis or squash racquets; and golf
clubs.

ⓘ As entry requirements and customs regulations are subject
to change, you should always check the current situation with
your local travel agent, airline or an Italian embassy or
consulate before you leave.

Driving in Naples is extraordinarily challenging due to the many restrictions to help combat the city's traffic congestion problems and air pollution. If you do decide to drive, try and book into a hotel with parking spots and spend your time either using public transport or walking. Not only will this allow you to see a lot more of the region, but also you'll get around a lot faster and avoid the parking headaches and chaotic driving associated with a stay in the city.

If you happen to break down, national motoring groups (AA or RAC in the UK, and the AAA/CAA in the US and Canada) have reciprocal agreements with the Automobile Club d'Italia (ACI).

ACI Piazzale Tecchio 49D ☎ 803 116 24-hr emergency line
🔟 www.aci.it

By bus

Long-distance buses connect Naples with most other European countries. Most travellers will have to change in Rome to reach their destination. The arrival point is outside the Stazione Centrale. From London by National Express, the fastest journey time is about 24 hours. 🔟 www.nationalexpress.com

ENTRY FORMALITIES

Visitors to Italy who are citizens of the UK, Ireland, Australia, the USA, Canada or New Zealand will need a passport, but not a visa for stays of up to three months. After that time they must apply for a *permesso di soggiorno* (permit to stay). If you are travelling from other countries, you may need a visa; it is best to check before you leave home.

MONEY

The currency in Italy is the euro. If you are coming from another country in the EU that uses the euro currency, you will not need to change money. A euro is divided into 100 cents. Currency denominations are: 50 euro, 20 euro, 10 euro, 5 euro, 2 euro, 1 euro, 50 cents, 20 cents, 10 cents, 5 cents and 1 cent. You can withdraw money using ATMs at many Italian banks.

The most widely accepted credit cards are Visa and MasterCard. American Express is less commonly permitted. Many smaller businesses – including some restaurants, taverns, smaller hotels and most market stalls – do not accept credit card payment. This is especially true outside Naples and the main tourist destinations.

ⓘ It is advisable to carry a small amount of cash to cover your day's purchases.

HEALTH, SAFETY & CRIME

It is not necessary to take any special health precautions while travelling in Italy. Tap water is safe to drink, but do not drink any water from surrounding lakes or rivers as the region is not known for its commitment to environmentalism. Many Italians prefer bottled mineral water, especially sparkling varieties.

As the region is quite arid and hilly, hiking is a popular pastime. If you do decide to go for a stroll, it is best to inform someone before you embark on your journey as conditions can change fast – especially at the top of Vesuvius. Heatstroke is also a common problem so don't go anywhere without appropriate clothing and ample water supplies.

Pharmacies (or *farmacias*) are marked by a large green or red cross. Italian pharmacists can provide informal medical advice on simple ailments. However, prescriptions will always cost more to fill than they would back home.

Italian health care is of a good standard, but is not free. In most cases your travel insurance should provide the coverage you need.

Crime has always been a problem in the city of Naples. Its reputation is far worse than reality. Petty theft (bag-snatching, pick-pocketing) is the most common form of trouble for tourists and activity is particularly high in the much-frequented historic sights. You are unlikely to experience violence or assault, which occur mainly in the context of gangland activities. Don't carry too much cash and avoid walking around late at night on badly lit streets (especially if you are a woman). Your hotel will warn you about particular areas to avoid.

When using public transport or walking on the street, carry your wallet in your front pocket, keep bags closed at all times, never leave valuables on the ground when you are seated at a table, and always wear camera cases and bags crossed over your chest.

For details of emergency numbers, refer to the 'Emergencies' section on page 154.

OPENING HOURS

Most businesses open 09.00–18.00 Monday to Friday. Retail shops stay open until 20.00 with a 2- to 3-hour lunch break starting around 13.30. Restaurants and cafés usually close between lunch and dinner sittings from 15.30 until 19.00. Most also remain closed for breakfast. Many companies close for large chunks of the month of August – except on the Amalfi Coast and on the islands of Capri, Ischia and Procida when the season is in full swing. Banks open 08.20–13.20, 14.45–15.45 Monday to Friday.

Cultural institutions usually close for one day per week – usually Monday or Tuesday. Only the biggest and most popular sights remain open seven days a week. Sundays will, however, have limited hours.

Usual post office opening hours are from 08.15–19.00 Mondays to Fridays and from 08.15–noon Saturdays .

TOILETS

There are very few public toilet facilities in Naples. The best approach is to use the toilet in a bar. You can usually walk straight in without having to buy a drink. If the bar is empty, it is a matter of politeness to ask the bartender first. In restaurants there may be signs saying that toilets are for use only by paying customers. Fast-food joints and department stores are other good options if you need a comfort break.

CHILDREN

Naples is generally a child-friendly city. Perfect strangers will dote over your little angels at every opportunity – but while local kids will often be spotted playing in the streets, your tots may not be as familiar with the rules of the road and will be unused to dealing with speeding Vespas and cars. Don't worry about bringing your children to a restaurant, as all will welcome their presence. Just don't expect any high chairs or 'kiddy' menus. Luckily, pasta dishes tend to go down well with fussy eaters.

If kids start to get bored, consider taking them to any of the following destinations to help them pass the time.

- **Beaches** City beaches are decidedly unclean and should be avoided at all costs. Your best bet is to head out of town to the

Amalfi Coast or to the outlying islands. The beaches here are small and rocky, so you will have to keep watch of your children at all times.

- **Funfair** Edenlandia is a traditional funfair with a host of ageing thrill-rides. Your kids will love it. ⓐ Viale Kennedy, Fuorigrotta ⓣ 081 239 4800 ⓛ 14.00–20.00 Tues–Fri, 10.30–midnight Sat & Sun, Apr, May; 17.00–midnight Mon–Fri, 10.30–midnight Sun, June, Sept; 17.00–midnight Mon–Sat, 10.30–midnight Sun, July, Aug; 10.30–midnight Sat & Sun Oct–Mar

- **Museums** The Città della Scienzia is a child-friendly museum of attractions, many of which are hands-on. Also inside is a Planetarium with showings throughout the day. A good place to go when the weather turns sour. ⓐ Via Coroglio 104 ⓣ 081 372 3728 ⓛ 09.00–17.00 Tues–Sat, 10.00–19.00 Sun

COMMUNICATIONS

Phones

Italian phone numbers need to be dialled with their area codes regardless of where you are calling from. All numbers in Naples and its province begin with 081. This includes Sorrento and the islands of Ischia, Capri and Procida. Amalfi and Ravello, located in the province of Salerno, have the code 089.

Phone numbers in Naples usually have seven digits. However, older establishments may have only six. All numbers beginning with 800 are toll-free. Mobile phone numbers always begin with 3.

Public phones in Naples tend to be at busy intersections. As a result, it can be a challenge hearing anything that is being said down the line. The plus side is that almost everyone in Naples has a mobile, so public phone booths are almost always available.

MAKING PHONE CALLS

❶ The minimum charge for a local call is 10 cents. You will need a phone card before you are permitted to make calls. These are available from any of the numerous *tabacchi*. Some public phones may also take credit cards – usually the phones at train stations and airports.

Post

Italy's post system is beginning to improve after decades of unreliability. Post boxes are red and have two slots divided between local destinations (*per la citta*) and everywhere else (*tutte le altre destinazioni*). Some also have a section with a blue sticker on the front for first-class post.

For post being sent out of the country, first class is the only choice you have. First-class service promises 24-hr delivery for any destination in Italy, and three days for anywhere in the EU. For anywhere else on the planet, keep your fingers crossed.

Letters less than 20 g to Italy or other EU countries cost 62 cents or 80 cents to the USA. Australian post costs €1. Registered mail starts at €2.80.

Internet

Most Italian phone lines now have sockets for RJ11 jacks, although some older lines will have sockets for large three-pin plugs. Broadband in hotels is still a bit of a luxury, unless you are staying in a major chain property. And if you yearn for wireless services, dream on. Internet cafés are scattered throughout the city – each one varying in speed. Try to choose a business centre in a hotel or a café with multiple terminals to ensure high-quality service.

ELECTRICITY

The standard electrical current is 220 volts. Two-pin adaptors can be purchased at most electrical shops.

TRAVELLERS WITH DISABILITIES

For people with disabilities, Naples is a notoriously difficult city to negotiate. Ask staff at the location you are visiting if they can help you, as there may be ramps that can be placed over stairs. In museums the ground floors are usually accessible, as are those in more modern galleries. Buses are completely wheelchair unfriendly. Try using the modern and efficient metro and overground trains instead. New metro stations have wheelchair access features (ramps and lifts) incorporated into the design. But even where ramps exist, you will often find them obstructed by cars or motorcycles. Lifts are often too small for a wheelchair to enter and the narrow, cobblestoned streets can be uncomfortable.

The historic sights of Pompeii and Herculaneum, while outdoors, are little better. Access to the actual collection of ruins may have ramps, but the pathways date back to the original Roman period and are littered with wheel ruts and cracks making manoeuvrability difficult.

Ⓦ www.sath.org (US-based site)

Ⓦ www.access-able.com (general advice on worldwide travel)

Ⓦ http://travel.guardian.co.uk (UK site offering tips and links for disabled travellers)

FURTHER INFORMATION

Three local tourist boards serve Naples. Each one provides maps and information of varying quality.

ASST ⓐ Via San Carlo 9 ⓣ 081 252 5711 ⓛ 09.00–13.30, 15.00–19.30 Mon–Fri, 09.00–14.00 Sat & Sun ⓝ Bus: 24, C57, E1, R1, R2. Other location at Piazza del Gesù

Ente Provinciale del Turismo (EPT) ⓐ Piazza dei Martiri ⓣ 081 410 7211 ⓛ 09.00–14.00 Mon–Fri ⓝ Bus: 140, C12, C18, C19, C24, C25, C28; Tram: 1, 4

Osservatorio Turistico-Culturale ⓐ Piazza del Plebiscito ⓣ 081 247 1123 ⓦ www.inaples.it ⓛ 09.00–19.00 Mon–Fri, 09.00–14.00 Sat ⓝ Bus: 140, C22, C25, E3, R2, R3

BACKGROUND READING

Georgics by Virgil. Classic work written by the ancient historian and poet while living in Naples.

The Bourbons of Naples by Harold Acton. Good chronicle of the reign of Ferdinand I.

See Naples and Die: The Camorra and Organised Crime by Tom Behan. A riveting account of the rise of the Camorra clans and their influence in Italian politics and society.

Pizza Napoletana! by Pamela Sheldon Johns. Everything you ever wanted to know about the history of pizza – and then some. It's worth getting your hands on a copy for the ten authentic pizza recipes from the city's finest establishments.

The Volcano Lover by Susan Sontag. Perfect holiday reading. Romantic, fictional take on the relationship between Lord Nelson and his mistress Emma Hamilton.

Cosi Fan Tutti by Michael Dibdin. Slick crime novel set in the seedier pockets of Naples featuring detective Aurelio Zen.

Italian Journey by Johann Wolfgang Goethe. Great descriptions of 18th-century Neapolitan life from the German philosopher. There are many versions, but the best features translations by W H Auden.

⬥ *Naples, a colourful and vibrant city*

Useful phrases

Although English is spoken in many tourist locations in Naples, these words and phrases may come in handy. See also the phrases for specific situations in other parts of this book.

English	Italian	Approx. pronunciation
BASICS		
Yes	Sì	See
No	No	Noh
Please	Per favore	Perr fahvawreh
Thank you	Grazie	Grahtsyeh
Hello	Salve	Sahlveh
Goodbye	Arrivederci	Arreevehderrchee
Excuse me	Scusi	Skoozee
Sorry	Scusi	Skoozee
That's okay	Va bene	Vah behneh
To	A	Ah
From	Da	Dah
I don't speak Italian	Non parlo italiano	Nawn parrlaw itahlyahnaw
Do you speak English?	Parla inglese?	Parrla eenglehzeh?
Good morning	Buon giorno	Booawn geeyawrnaw
Good afternoon	Buon pomeriggio	Booawn pawmehreehdjaw
Good evening	Buonasera	Booawnah sehrah
Goodnight	Buonanotte	Booawnah nawtteh
My name is ...	Mi chiamo ...	Mee kyahmaw ...
DAYS & TIMES		
Monday	Lunedì	Loonehdee
Tuesday	Martedì	Marrtehdee
Wednesday	Mercoledì	Merrcawlehdee
Thursday	Giovedì	Jawvehdee
Friday	Venerdì	Venerrdee
Saturday	Sabato	Sahbahtaw
Sunday	Domenica	Dawmehneeca
Morning	Mattino	Mahtteenaw
Afternoon	Pomeriggio	Pawmehreedjaw
Evening	Sera	Sehra
Night	Notte	Notteh
Yesterday	Ieri	Yeree

English	Italian	Approx. pronunciation
Today	Oggi	Odjee
Tomorrow	Domani	Dawmahnee
What time is it?	Che ore sono?	Keh awreh sawnaw?
It is ...	Sono le ...	Sawnaw leh ...
09.00	Nove	Noveh
Midday	Mezzogiorno	Metsawjorrnaw
Midnight	Mezzanotte	Metsanotteh

NUMBERS

One	Uno	Oonaw
Two	Due	Dweh
Three	Tre	Treh
Four	Quattro	Kwahttraw
Five	Cinque	Cheenkweh
Six	Sei	Say
Seven	Sette	Setteh
Eight	Otto	Ottaw
Nine	Nove	Noveh
Ten	Dieci	Dyehchee
Eleven	Undici	Oondeechee
Twelve	Dodici	Dawdeechee
Twenty	Venti	Ventee
Fifty	Cinquanta	Cheenkwahnta
One hundred	Cento	Chentaw

MONEY

I would like to change these traveller's cheques/this currency	Vorrei cambiare questi assegni turistici/ questa valuta	Vawrray cahmbyahreh kwestee assenee tooree- steechee/kwesta vahloota
Where is the nearest ATM?	Dov'è il bancomat più vicino?	Dawveh eel bankomaht pyoo veecheenaw?
Do you accept credit cards?	Accettate carte di credito?	Achetahteh kahrrteh dee krehdeehtaw?

SIGNS & NOTICES

Airport	Aeroporto	Ahaerrhawpawrrtaw
Railway station	Stazione ferroviaria	Stahtsyawneh ferrawvyarya
Platform	Binario	Binahriaw
Smoking/ non-smoking	Per fumatori/ non fumatori	Perr foomahtawree/ non foomahtawree
Toilets	Gabinetti	Gabinetteh
Ladies/Gentlemen	Signore/Signori	Seenyawreh/Seenyawree
Subway	Metropolitana	Metrawpawleetahna

Emergencies

EMERGENCY NUMBERS
Ambulance 118
Carabineri (national/military police) 112
Car breakdown 803 116
Fire brigade 115
Polizia di Stato (national police) 113

MEDICAL EMERGENCIES
If you need a doctor or dentist during your stay, then check out the local English *Yellow Pages*. The directory will list English-speaking practitioners. If you can't get your hands on this guide, then your hotel concierge and/or the local tourist office should have a list of possibilities.

For serious emergencies, go directly to the emergency departments of either of the two major hospitals in town (see page 155).

Two dentists with English speaking staff are:
Dottore Francesco Oliveri ❷ Via Carducci 6 ❶ 081 245 7003
Dottore Massimo Palmieri ❷ Via G Orsi 8 ❶ 081 566 3721

Emergency pharmacy
Pharmacies (or *farmacias*) are marked by a green or red cross. Over-the-counter drugs are more expensive in Italy than they are in the UK or USA. Most pharmacies keep standard business hours, which are ❶ 8.30–13.00, 16.00–20.00 Mon–Fri and 8.30–13.00 Sat. It is the law that a sign needs to be posted by the front door pointing customers to the nearest late-opening pharmacy.

Hospitals
Cardarelli ⓐ Via Cardarelli 9 ☎ 081 747 1111
Santobono ⓐ Via M Fiore 6 ☎ 081 220 5111

🔺 *Mounted police in the Centro Storico*

POLICE

Crimes can be reported to either the Carabineri or Commissariati.

Questura Centrale (Police headquarters) ⓐ Via Medina 75
ⓣ 081 794 1111

STOLEN & LOST PROPERTY

If you lose anything or suspect that it has been stolen, then go straight to the nearest police station. While there, you will need to make a *denuncia* statement. If the loss occurred while on the train, then go to the *ufficio oggetti rivenuti* (ⓣ 081 567 4660) on platform 24 of the Stazione Centrale.

Metro thefts and losses need to be reported at the office located at the terminus of the line you were riding. If that's impossible, try calling the helpline on ⓣ 800 639 525. The office is open from 08.30–18.00 Mon–Fri. For items left on the SITA bus system, ⓣ 081 552 2176. Finally, the lost property office at the airport (ⓣ 081 789 6237) is open from 07.00–24.00 every day.

CONSULATES & EMBASSIES

Australian Embassy ⓐ Via Antonio Bosio 5, Rome ⓣ 06 852 721
ⓦ www.italy.embassy.gov.au

British Consulate-General ⓐ Via dei Mille 40 ⓣ 081 423 8911
ⓦ www.britain.it ⓛ 09.00–12.30, 14.00–16.00 Mon–Fri; times change slightly in summer

Canadian Consulate-General ⓐ Via G Carducci 29 ⓣ 081 401 338
ⓛ 09.00–13.00 Mon–Fri

New Zealand Embassy ⓐ Via Zara 28, Rome ⓣ 06 441 7171
ⓦ www.nzembassy.com

ⓞ *Keeping up with the news*

Republic of Ireland Embassy @ Piazza di Campitelli 3, Rome
ℹ 06 697 9121 🌐 http://foreignaffairs.gov.ie
Republic of South Africa Embassy @ Via Tanaro 14, Rome ℹ 06 852
541 🌐 www.sudafrica.it
US Consulate-General @ Piazza della Repubblica ℹ 081 583 8111
🌐 www.usembassy.it 🕐 08.00–13.00, 14.00–17.00 Mon–Fri

EMERGENCY PHRASES

Help! Aiuto! *Ahyootaw!*   **Fire!** Al fuoco! *Ahl fooawcaw!*
Stop! Ferma! *Fairmah!*

Call an ambulance/a doctor/the police/the fire service!
Chiamate un'ambulanza/un medico/la polizia/i pompieri!
*Kyahmahteh oon ahmboolahntsa/oon mehdeecaw/la
pawleetsya/ee pompee-ehree!*

INDEX

ACKNOWLEDGEMENTS & FEEDBACK

The publishers would like to thank Neil Setchfield for supplying the copyright photos for this book.

Copy editor: Sandra Stafford
Proofreader: Lynn Bresler

Send your thoughts to
books@thomascook.com

- **Found a great bar, club, shop or must-see sight that we don't feature?**

- **Like to tip us off about any information that needs updating?**

- **Want to tell us what you love about this handy little guidebook and more importantly how we can make it even handier?**

Then here's your chance to tell all! Send us ideas, discoveries and recommendations today and then look out for your valuable input in the next edition of this title. As an extra 'thank you' from Thomas Cook Publishing, you'll be automatically entered into our exciting monthly prize draw.

Send an email to the above address (stating the book's title) or write to: CitySpots Project Editor, Thomas Cook Publishing, PO Box 227, The Thomas Cook Business Park, Unit 18, Coningsby Road, Peterborough PE3 8SB, UK.